The Future of the People of God

The Future of the People of God

Reading Romans Before and After
Western Christendom

ANDREW PERRIMAN

CASCADE *Books* • Eugene, Oregon

THE FUTURE OF THE PEOPLE OF GOD
Reading Romans Before and After Western Christendom

Copyright © 2010 Andrew Perriman. All rights reserved. Except for brief quotations
in critical publications or reviews, no part of this book may be reproduced in any
manner without prior written permission from the publisher. Write: Permissions,
Wipf and Stock Publishers, 199 W. 8th Ave., Suite 3, Eugene, OR 97401.

Cascade Books
An imprint of Wipf and Stock Publishers
199 W. 8th Ave., Suite 3
Eugene, OR 97401
www.wipfandstock.com

ISBN 13: 978-1-60608-787-9

Unless otherwise indicated, all Scripture quotations are from The Holy Bible, English
Standard Version, published by HarperCollins Publishers © 2001 by Crossway
Bibles, a division of Good News Publishers. Used by Permission. All rights reserved.

Septuagint quotations, unless otherwise indicated, are from *A New English
Translation of the Septuagint*, ©2007 by the International Organization for
Septuagint and Cognate Studies, Inc. Used by permission of Oxford University Press.
All rights reserved.

Cataloging-in-Publication data:

Perriman, Andrew.

The future of the people of God : reading Romans before and after western
Christendom / Andrew Perriman.

viii + 180 p. ; 23 cm. — Includes bibliographical references and indexes.

ISBN 13: 978-1-60608-787-9

1. Bible. N.T. Romans—Criticism, interpretation, etc. I. Author.

BS2665.2 P48 2010

Manufactured in the U.S.A.

For Linus, thankful to have been
part of—and to have been inspired by—his Great Expedition

Contents

Abbreviations

2 *Bar.*	*2 Baruch (Syriac Apocalypse)*
1 *En.*	*1 Enoch (Ethiopic Apocalypse)*
1 Esd	1 Esdras
Eusebius *Hist. eccl.*	Eusebius, *Historia ecclesiastica*
Eusebius *Vit. Const.*	Eusebius, *Vita Constantini*
Ign. *Rom.*	Ignatius, *To the Romans*
Jos. Asen.	*Joseph and Aseneth*
Josephus *Ag. Ap.*	Josephus, *Against Apion*
Josephus *Ant.*	Josephus, *Jewish Antiquities*
Josephus *J. W.*	Josephus, *Jewish War*
Jub.	*Jubilees*
LCL	Loeb Classical Library
1–2 Macc	1–2 Maccabees
3–4 Macc	3–4 Maccabees
Mart. Pol.	*Martyrdom of Polycarp*
NPNF²	Nicene and Post-Nicene Fathers, Series 2
OGIS	*Orientis Graecis Inscriptiones Selectae.* 2 vols. Edited by W. Dittenberger. Leipzig, 1903–05; repr. New York, 1970.
Pol. *Phil.*	Polycarp, *To the Philippians*
Ps-Philo *Lib. Ant.*	*Liber antiquitatum biblicarum* (Pseudo-Philo)
Pss. Sol.	*Psalms of Solomon*
Sib. Or.	*Sibylline Oracles*
Sir	Sirach/Ecclesiasticus
Suetonius *Cal.*	Suetonius, *Gaius Caligula*
Suetonius *Claud.*	Suetonius, *Claudius*
T. Levi	*Testament of Levi*
Tacitus *Ann.*	Tacitus, *Annales*
Wis	Wisdom of Solomon

1

[handwritten: christians blamed for Nero's fire, tortured -64]

Reading Romans Before Christendom

> Simply said, it was time for the gods of that age to withdraw: for
> too long they had served as the terrible and beautiful guardians
> of an order of majestic cruelty and pitiless power; for too long
> they had not only received oblations and bestowed blessings but
> had presided over and consecrated an empire of crucifixions and
> martial terror.[1]

It is usually reckoned that Paul wrote his letter to those called "saints"
in Rome (Rom 1:7), probably from Corinth, around AD 55–56, a year
or two after the accession of Nero. There was nothing very inauspicious
about the early years of Nero's reign and no obvious reason for Paul to be
concerned about the security of the churches in the city. But that would
change dramatically within a decade. On the night of 18–19 July AD
64, according to Tacitus's well-known account (Tacitus *Ann.* 15.44; cf.
Suetonius *Nero* 16.2), fire broke out in shops containing flammable goods
at the southeastern end of the Circus Maximus. Blown by the wind the
blaze raced through the combustible wooden structures of the congested
lower parts of the city and then spread to the hills. It burned for days. Of
the fourteen districts that made up Rome only four escaped unscathed,
three were completely razed, and the remaining seven were left with only
a few half-intact, smoldering buildings. The historian does not attempt
to calculate the numbers of private mansions, tenement blocks, and
temples that were lost, but of the most prestigious temples he lists one
dedicated to Luna, the great altar and shrine built for Hercules, the temple

---

1. Hart, *Atheist Delusions*, 100–101.

of Jupiter, and the sanctuary of Vesta, which housed the tutelary deities of the Roman people.

Tacitus records—and apparently shared—the widespread belief that the emperor himself was responsible for the conflagration, his vainglorious intention being to found a magnificent new city bearing his name. He notes, for example, that attempts to stop the fire, which broke out on property belonging to the imperial family, were hampered by mischief-makers who claimed to have been authorized to make sure that it took its course; and a rumor had spread that while the city was burning, Nero took to a private stage in Antium and gaily sang of the destruction of Troy. In any case, the emperor took the opportunity, first, to construct for himself a splendid new palace and, secondly, to undertake a program of massive and very costly urban regeneration, stimulated by lavish donations from his own pocket.

The next task was to propitiate the gods. The Sibylline books gave direction that prayers should be offered to Vulcanus, Ceres, and Proserpina. The matrons of the city made entreaties to the goddess Juno, and married women held banquets and vigils. But neither Nero's munificence nor the many official acts of piety succeeded in dispelling the sinister suspicion that the fire had been started deliberately. So in a last attempt to put an end to the report, Nero fixed the blame on a "class of men, loathed for their vices, whom the crowd styled Christians." These reprobates took their name from a certain Christus, who had been executed by the governor of Judea during the reign of Tiberius. Following his death a "pernicious superstition" had broken out in Palestine and had since spread to Rome, "where all things horrible or shameful in the world collect and find a vogue." Arrests were quickly made, and large numbers of Christians were convicted, not so much of setting fire to the city as of "hatred of the human race." Their punishment was theatrical and grotesque. They were torn apart by dogs, nailed to crosses, or burned as torches in Nero's garden to illuminate the spectacle. Tacitus had little sympathy for these godless malefactors, but even he was shocked by the savagery of the pogrom: "they were being sacrificed not for the welfare of the state but to the ferocity of a single man."

[handwritten: • must look at historical content]

Romans as an Eschatological Text

[handwritten: • Paul knew judgment was coming to Israel]
[handwritten: • knew Gospel would bring suffering]

This may seem an odd, anachronistic, and distracting point from which
to begin a reading of Romans; but there are two respects in which I think
this story will get us moving in the right direction. First, we will do well
to keep in mind, as we work our way through a letter that has much to
say about persecution and suffering, that *Romans is a historical text with a
historical frame of reference*—and that arguably this terrifying horizon of a
great Day of Fire should have no less relevance for interpretation than the
destruction of Jerusalem has for understanding Jesus's life and teaching.
Indeed, it was only two years after the fire that the ill-fated revolt against
the imperial occupying power broke out in Judea, which resulted in the
destruction of Jerusalem and the temple, and, if we can trust Josephus's
arithmetic, the death of more than a million Jews. Given that Paul presents
himself as an apostle called to proclaim and interpret the resurrection of
Israel's Messiah to the nations (Rom 1:4–5), we must surely reckon with
the likelihood that certain critical, forward-looking trajectories in the letter will also land here. It seems to me virtually inconceivable that Paul—a
man clearly imbued with the mindset of the prophets—could have used
the language of the Old Testament to speak about wrath against the Jews
and not have imagined some such outcome. Secondly, the story reminds
us how precarious the existence of the early communities of believers was
in an inhospitable world dominated by the pagan gods and subject to
the savage and unaccountable foibles of the ruling elite. I believe that we
do the apostles a great disservice if we suppose that this situation was
only of marginal interest to them and not a matter of central and urgent
concern.

These two observations, in a preliminary way, define the scope of
this book. What I will suggest is that Paul's argument in Romans in effect presupposes—in a way that is critical for interpretation—a narrative
about the concrete existence of the "people of God," that runs, roughly
speaking, from the exile as a paradigmatic judgment on Israel, through
the painful experience of subjugation by foreign powers, including the
disastrous war of AD 66–73, through a traumatic bifurcation set in mo-
tion by Jesus and his followers, through a period of intense conflict with
the paganism of the Greco-Roman *oikoumenē* (more on the scope of this

term in chapter 5), to reach a provisional but nonetheless momentous conclusion in a victory over the gods and nations of the old world, represented most clearly by Constantine's *deliverance* of the churches from persecution and the subsequent *elevation* of Christianity to the status of imperial religion by Theodosius. The point is not that Paul foresaw with any great clarity or precision what would be the historical consequences of his "gospel"—and certainly not that he foresaw what lay beyond the horizon of the birth of Christendom. But we will have to reckon with the fact that his argument in Romans about the righteousness of God is geared towards future events that were to have a decisive impact both on the Jew and on the Greek, both on believers and on unbelievers; and that we are likely to distort both his theology and his practical instruction with regard to the life of the community if we lose sight of the concrete political and social reality of these events.

In other words, we will have to reckon with the fact that Romans is an *eschatological* text—not in the idealized, popular, end-of-the-world sense, but in the sense that it addresses the concrete existence of the churches in Rome in the light of foreseen events that would be pivotal for the future identity and security of the people of God. The framing historical narrative has been, for the most part, suppressed by the theologies of Christendom because, for all their disagreements, they have operated from the premise that the final interpretive context for New Testament thought has been established in its assimilation to European rationalism. So all that is merely historical may be stripped away to leave the naked, shivering body of theological and devotional truth. We now have serious doubts, however, about the integrity and reliability of the overarching meta-narrative of Christendom; and if our own story as the modern—or postmodern—church can be relativized in this way, we may begin to see the value, not only for biblical interpretation but also for the current task of ecclesial and missional redefinition, of relocating New Testament thought in a limiting historical narrative. By setting a provisional historical horizon to our reading of the text, we allow ourselves both to give proper consideration to the contingency and realism of Paul's argument and to rethink our own critical historical context.

A Hubbub of Voices

[handwritten margin notes: • Paul uses OT to make arguments • most look at conversation between OT and NT • controversy between Jews and ... covenant major issue new]

There is also a literary dimension to the contextualization of Romans that will be extremely important for interpretation. In the first place, Paul's argument about the gospel of God and its significance for the churches of the nations is constructed to a large degree from materials salvaged from the Old Testament in the form of quotation or allusion. We will assume as we read the text that Paul has done this with what we might now call a critical awareness of the larger argumentative or narrative context from which the quotation or allusion is drawn, and that this context is likely to be, in one way or another, *determinative* for his own argument. To give an example that will be immediately relevant for us: we cannot make sense of Paul's quotation of Habakkuk 2:4 in Romans 1:17 ("The righteous shall live by faith") without first bringing into detailed focus the extensive prophetic argument about the dilemma faced by the few "righteous" in Israel from which the quotation has been clipped, and then asking how Paul makes use of this whole narrative, and not merely the isolated aphorism, to interpret the situation faced by the community in Rome. As a trope this is sometimes called metalepsis, though to explain it, as Hays does, in terms of the "allusive echo" that is generated in the "unstated or suppressed . . . points of resonance between the two texts" rather understates the argumentative or narrative force that it carries in Paul.[2]

However, the Jewish Scriptures constitute only one aspect of the literary environment that has shaped the language and thought of Romans. It will become apparent, as we attend to the overtones of the text, that the argument is the product—both substantially and rhetorically, and probably quite deliberately—of the intense and troubled engagement with first-century Judaism that resulted from the apostolic activity that is outlined in the letter. We should hear a hubbub of Jewish voices ringing in our ears, and we should not fool ourselves into believing that we will read the text better by filtering out the noise. John Piper advises "scholars and pastors and laypeople who do not spend much of their time reading first-century literature" to exercise some skepticism towards arguments such as N. T. Wright's about *euangelion* that attribute a novel sense to familiar terminology on the basis of literary and historical context.[3] That is

2. Hays, *Echoes*, 20.
3. Piper, *Future*, 36.

retrogressive advice: the familiarity is precisely the problem, and the need is for "scholars and pastors and laypeople" to get out more—that is, out of the very small literary and linguistic world of the biblical text into the fascinating and enlivening environment that gave birth to it. Of course, the effect can be generated only to a limited degree: we cannot immerse ourselves in the thought-world of Paul's various audiences. But as far as is possible, we will attempt to reconstruct narratives and arguments—both from the Old Testament and from the major works known to us from Second Temple Judaism—in the expectation that this will bring out the rich contextual dynamic of Paul's thought. If it feels at times as though we are wading knee-deep through intertextual mud, then I suggest that that is a good thing—the nearest we can get to the experience of total immersion.

The Shape of Things to Come *Persecuted → dominant → contested*

must understand Romans through Paul's eye)

big picture: God's dominance Israel's Churches)

Nero's persecution of the Christians in a blatantly dishonest attempt to appease either the gods or the people was simply an early sensational flare-up in what was to be a long, arduous, and bloody conflict between an emerging counterculture of Jewish origins and the old pagan order. The climax would come with the Great Persecution under Diocletian in the early years of the fourth century. The persecution lasted for ten years and was brought officially to an end by the Edict of Milan in AD 313, which marked—at least in symbolic terms—the triumph of Christ over the gods of the Greek and Roman world. The significance of the moment is captured in the speech later made by the recusant emperor Licinius while sacrificing in a grove—albeit a speech disingenuously concocted for him by the church historian Eusebius (c. AD 260–339)—in which he portrays the coming engagement with Constantine as a final show-down between the old gods of Rome and the "strange God" of the Christians: "Suppose, then, this strange God, whom we now regard with ridicule, should really prove victorious; then indeed we must acknowledge and give him honor, and so bid a long farewell to those for whom we light our tapers in vain. But if our own gods triumph (as they undoubtedly will), then, as soon as we have secured the present victory, let us prosecute the war without delay against these despisers of the gods" (Eusebius *Vit. Const.* 2.5, NPNF²).

God beat gods. ruled world now threatens

Licinius lost the battle, and the strange, ambitious God of Abraham and the patriarchs came to ascendancy across the empire under the name of Jesus Christ—a victory achieved through the extraordinary faithfulness of a people so passionately attached to Christ that they were willing to suffer and die with him in order to be glorified with him.

That ascendancy lasted for many centuries in one form or another, but it has now more or less evaporated. Very few people today regard Europe as a Christian continent other than in a residual cultural sense. Yes, the church appears to be flourishing outside Europe, not least where it has had to emulate the faithfulness of the early communities in their subjection to the cruel antipathy of the old pagan world; and the re-importation of this vigorous faith into the West may—or may not—have a significant revitalizing effect. But there must be some suspicion that the current form of global Christianity carries the same genetic susceptibility to irrelevance and decay under modern conditions, and that it will not have the resources to deal, in any credible public way, with the massive challenge that an aggressively secular and pluralist culture now poses to the Christian worldview.

I take it as a rough guiding hypothesis, therefore, 1) that the church faces a massive, and insufficiently understood, crisis of identity and purpose on all levels as a consequence of having been unceremoniously and sometimes quite contemptuously sidelined by the dominant culture of the West; 2) that this marginalization is self-evident in Europe, but in the long run is likely to be no less of a challenge for the ostensibly stronger global church; 3) that we will not in the end grasp the seriousness of the problem, or find answers to it, by framing it in terms of polarities internal to the Christendom mindset: between ancient and modern, between divergent Reformation traditions, between mainstream and dissident or conservative and liberal theologies; 4) that we need to address critically the entire legacy of the Christendom phenomenon, from the first rewriting of the biblical narrative in the language and thought-forms of the Greeks, through the long ages of cultural domination and slow decline, to the increasingly desperate endeavors to conserve, commandeer, deconstruct and reinvent that we are confronted with today; 5) that in order to imagine a viable future for the people of God in a rapidly mutating culture we need, in the first place, to reconsider how the New Testament reads as a narrative-historical and theological precursor to the emergence

Cure identity crisis by reading NT as historical narrative and precursor of today

of Christendom) and finally 6) that this hermeneutic is likely to lead both to a more coherent and plausible understanding of Scripture and to a far-reaching reconstruction of the theological identity and practical purpose of the church for the age to come.

It is the point about re-imagining a viable future for the people of God that makes Romans such a pertinent text for the church today. I will argue that in order to read Romans *after* Christendom we must first read it *before* Christendom, as a text that anticipates the real-world victory of Christ over the manifold gods of the nations. That is not an easy conceptual shift to make. On the one hand, for many of us the reality—or at least the reputation—of Christendom has left a bad taste in the mouth, and we naturally resist the suggestion that the political, cultural, and religious hegemony of the church in Europe and in the world colonized and dominated by the European powers might be seen as the fulfillment of the New Testament hope that Christ would come to rule the nations. On the other hand, the intellectual transformation of biblical thought that has sustained this hegemony right up until the modern era has largely persuaded us that the writers of the New Testament were incapable of contemplating the future in contingent and limited terms, as the simple continuation of history. The assumption is that if Jesus has been elevated to the defining pinnacle of the cosmos, every conclusion drawn from that must have cosmic significance; if the Word of God has triumphed over the wisdom of the Greeks, then its various dogmatic pronouncements must have universal validity.

But Paul did not suffer from the benefit of our hindsight. He contemplated the future from the perspective of a Jew who understood the hope expressed by the Old Testament prophets that the nations would eventually acknowledge the sovereignty of YHWH, who had encountered the risen Christ as the embodiment of the persecuted churches (Acts 9:1–4; 22:3–8; 26:9–15), who had experienced firsthand the fearful hostility of both Jews and pagans towards those who dared to proclaim Christ; and, not surprisingly, he looked forward to a time when, for the sake of the glory of Israel's God and for the sake of the churches, the current state of affairs would be overturned. He believed that the day would come when his God would be *publicly* vindicated and shown to be righteous, when those who had taken the risky step of trusting in this God would be *publicly* vindicated and shown to be on the right side of history.

Less Is More - Israel must be judged first in.
- God made Jesus the vindery

I think we can also assume—and I think it can be shown—that even in a highly theological text such as Romans Paul's argument remains locked into what is essentially a historical narrative about the concrete existence of a community, punctuated by certain critical events. Because the narrative is bounded both geopolitically and temporally, because it *precedes* the fulfillment that came to be interpreted in accordance with the overweening intellectual self-confidence of Western civilization, we would do well to disable the universalizing assumptions that we bring to the text and, in the interests of exegesis, re-contextualize ourselves—to the point that we come to share Paul's necessarily myopic outlook and limited horizon, to the point that the fate of national Israel matters more to us than the theoretical relationship of the Law to faith, to the point that we are more troubled by the prospect of a pagan backlash than by the suspicion that others have not rightly understood justification theory.

A central argument will be that Paul's gospel of the resurrected "Son of God" has in view a decisive judgment not of the whole cosmos or all humanity but of the Greco-Roman world, which will result in the public (and political) "vindication" of the marginalized God of Israel. For God to be righteous in that judgment, however, he must first hold Israel accountable—not least because in the long run it will be through the faithful witness of his people that the old order of things will be overturned. Since Israel has proved itself to be as much in captivity to sin as the rest of humanity, the verdict on the nation must be destruction—and destruction of the sort that Jesus predicted. But God has put forward in advance of his eventual vindication in the world, in advance of a concrete victory over the gods of the nations, the story of Jesus's death and resurrection. In the existence of the eschatological community that is *in Jesus*, that has chosen the narrow path leading to life, that participates both in his dying and in his resurrection, there is the ground for the hope that the family of Abraham will realistically inherit the world. Paul takes trouble, therefore, to account for the foreseen sufferings of the saints in Rome in relation to an eschatological narrative that will climax in the vindication of those who, like Jesus himself, are "sons of God"; and he provides practical instruction on how they should live specifically in the light of that narrative. This contextualized reading sets limits to the dogmatic and pastoral

9

significance of the letter, but it opens up some interesting possibilities for exploring what it means to be the people of God when it is no longer possible (or desirable) to represent the victory of YHWH over the gods of the nations through the various forms of political, social, and cultural dominance that made up Christendom.

So we will set out to read Romans carefully, attentive to historically relevant perspectives and structures of thought, which may be quite different to the perspectives and structures imposed by later debates. This is not a work of formal exegesis or fully annotated scholarship—it is not a *commentary* on Romans, and the reader should not expect to find every difficult interpretive decision assiduously mapped and resolved. It is primarily an attempt to capture something of the energy and narrative dynamic of the letter, to read it from a different point of view—even to renew the critical mind and imagination that we bring as committed readers to the text; and to a large extent it is at this level of rhetorical, literary, and historical coherence that the thesis asks, for now, to be evaluated.

Broadly speaking I follow the New Perspective in its rejection of the various Reformation lenses through which Romans has been read and by which interpreters have strained their eyes, in its sensitivity to historical and literary context, and in its concern to recover the very Jewish particularity of Paul's thought. But the New Perspective, in my view, has not had the courage of its hermeneutical convictions. So Daniel Kirk is right to say, "Once we have allowed the particularity of Israel's story to contextualize the identity of God and the quality of God's righteousness, we are forced to reconsider Romans as a whole."[4] But the question is then whether or at what point or by what transformation the particularity of Israel's story becomes the *universalized* story about Jesus as it has been told by the church. For all the rhetorical panache and the heady whiff of subversion that empire-critical studies have brought to the party, it has hardly been demonstrated from the texts that Paul can be coherently recast as an anti-imperial, proto-Marxist theorist. But they have at least exposed the extent to which we still struggle to understand how Paul's good news about a resurrected "Son of God" would have been heard within the ancient world. To evoke a scene that I think has a significant bearing on how we read Romans, we must ask what was going through Paul's mind, what story was he telling, what sort of outcomes did he envisage, when

4. Kirk, *Unlocking Romans*, 5.

he stood on the Areopagus and informed the bemused Athenians that his God would no longer turn a blind eye to their ignorance but now called them to repent, for "he has fixed a day on which he will judge the *oikoumenēn* in righteousness by a man whom he has appointed" (Acts 17:31)? What sort of line is to be drawn between this audacious announcement and the words of the Christian priest Isidore of Pelusium in Egypt, in about AD 420, quoted by Peter Brown in *The Rise of Western Christendom*: the "religion of the Greeks, made dominant for so many years, by such pains, by the expenditure of so much wealth, and by such feats of arms, has vanished from the earth"?[5]

- must read Romans as it was originally written to understand it in the context of todays world
- ultimate battle of God over gods
- judgment of Israel
- foreseen suffering
- dilemma of new covenant and Israel
- Pauls concern for Israels salvation
- Pauls concern for gentile salvation

It's about God being the God of all and saving His people

5. *Letter* 1270, *Patrologia Graeca* 78: 344A, cited in Brown, *Western Christendom*, 72.

2

The Apostle to the Nations and the Gospel of God

- God will save Israel before all nations
- Paul fulfilling mission to gentiles
- instructing catholics

There are two brief passages in which Paul discusses his intentions with regard to the "saints" in Rome—"saints" being a loaded and thematically significant term, not merely a pious substitute for "Christians," as will become apparent. In chapter 1 he speaks of the considerable frustration that he has experienced in not having been able to travel to Rome sooner. It has long been his desire to impart some "spiritual gift to strengthen you." Then he appears to correct himself, perhaps out of deference to a community which he did not himself found—"that is, that we may be *mutually* encouraged by each other's faith, both yours and mine" (Rom 1:11–12). The reason that he hopes to "have some fruit" (my translation) among them as he has had among the other nations is that he is under obligation to all peoples to make known to them the good news (1:13–15).

He returns to this theme towards the end of the letter. Clearly sensing a need again to justify what might be regarded as presumption on his part in writing to them, he takes some care to define the purpose and scope of his work as an apostle. First, he locates it within an Old Testament narrative about the salvation of Israel: he is the one who presents the suffering servant of YHWH to those who have not been informed, who have not heard, so that many nations will be astonished at him and "kings shall shut their mouth" (Rom 15:21; cf. Isa 52:15 LXX). Behind this is the argument from Scripture, which properly concludes Paul's practical instruction about bearing with the "failings of the weak" (15:1), that Christ became a "servant to the circumcised" in order to confirm the promises made to the fathers and in order that the nations might "glorify God for

12

his mercy" (15:8–9). Here we have the elegant biblical rationale that de-termines one aspect, at least, of Paul's mission: when God acts to redeem Israel in accordance with the promises made to the fathers, the event is to be publicized amongst the nations in order that they may glorify God for his mercy towards his people.

This is the force of the *catena* of quotations in Romans 15:8–12. Because God has saved him, delivering him from his enemies, making him head above the nations, David "will praise you, O Lord, among the nations, and sing to your name" (Ps 18:43–50). The nations will rejoice with Israel because God "will avenge the blood of his sons and take re-venge and repay the enemies with a sentence" (Deut 32:43 LXX). The nations are exhorted to praise the Lord, the God of Israel, "because his mercy became strong toward us" (Ps 116:1–2 LXX). Finally, Paul quotes Isaiah 11:10: "The root of Jesse will come, even he who arises to rule the Gentiles; in him will the Gentiles hope" (Rom 15:12). The thought of a rule over the nations is new here, but the distinction remains: the Gentiles come to hope in the one who has been appointed to rule *over restored Israel.* The "shoot from the stump of Jesse," filled with the Spirit of God, will judge the poor of the land with righteousness, he will defeat the wicked, he will bring peace to the transformed microcosm of Israel; and the "dispersed of Judah" will be gathered from the four corners of the earth.[1] So when Paul then prays for his—we assume—predominantly Gentile audience in Rome that the God of hope may "fill you with all joy and peace *in believing,* so that by the power of the Holy Spirit you may abound in hope" (15:13), he means in believing *that the God of Israel has acted to judge and deliver his people.*

Secondly, Paul sets his intention to visit the saints in Rome in the context of the larger itinerary of his apostolic career. He has so far ful-filled his calling to bring about the "obedience of the nations" (*hypakoēn ethnōn*) from Jerusalem to Illyricum (roughly modern Croatia). No longer having "place" (*topos*) in these regions, he plans to travel to Spain, with a stopover in Rome to enjoy the company of the believers there and be sent on his way by them. In the meantime, however, he is about to travel to

---

1. If we accept "earth" rather than "land" in Isaiah 11:4, the point is still that the "root of Jesse" will "strike the earth" for the sake of Israel. Watts thinks that "my holy mountain" in 11:9 "parallels *the earth* and implies the totality of God's redeemed and re-created world"; "earth" rather than "land" is justified by the parallel with "sea" (Watts, *Isaiah 1–33,* 173).

Jerusalem with the money that has been raised from the Gentile churches in Macedonia and Achaia "for the poor among the saints at Jerusalem"—a risky undertaking for which he solicits their prayers (15:17–32).

We can reasonably assume, therefore, that part of Paul's motivation in writing this letter was simply to give an account of his intentions with regard to the churches in Rome. In passing, however, he touches on a more substantive purpose. Having expressed his confidence that the saints in Rome are "full of goodness, filled with all knowledge and able to instruct one another" (15:14), he explains that he has nevertheless written to them rather boldly on some points—if only by way of reminder—because he considers it his singular responsibility as a "minister of Christ Jesus to the Gentiles in the priestly service of the gospel of God" to ensure that the offering of the nations is "acceptable (*euprosdektos*), sanctified by the Holy Spirit" (15:15–16).

The important observation to make here is that this statement concludes a section of practical teaching regarding the life of the church that began with the emphatic appeal to the "brothers," in similar cultic language, to "present your bodies as a living sacrifice, holy and acceptable (*euareston*) to God, which is your spiritual worship" (Rom 12:1).[2] Thus the only *explicit* reason that Paul gives for writing is to encourage them to take seriously the fact that as a community they constitute a "living sacrifice," an offering of the nations to the God of Israel in fulfillment of eschatological expectations. They are to be deferential towards one another as members of the same body (12:3–8); they should be supportive of one another under persecution (12:9–13); they should love their enemies and not seek to avenge themselves (12:14–21); they should endeavor to live at peace with the governing authorities (13:1–10); they should be prepared for the coming day (13:11–14); and the strong in faith should be respectful of those who are weak (14:1–15:6). All this is embraced by the metaphor of the sacrificial community. It is summed up in the example of Christ, who made himself a servant to Israel in order that the promise made to Abraham would not come to nothing and that the nations might glorify God for his mercy towards his people.

---

2. Dunn quotes Dahl: "Neither the similarity nor the difference between the formulations in 12:1 and 15:16 can be accidental" (Dunn, *Romans 9–16*, 861). The links between Paul's stated purpose in writing and the introduction of the parenetic material is reinforced by the repetition of the phrase "by the grace given to me" (Rom 12:3; 15:15).

The Apostle to the Nations and the Gospel of God

*• Presentation of Paul
• constant fight Jews
• esp Romans stayed true*

The Long Story behind the Offering of the Nations

That accounts for the material in Romans 12:1—15:13, but what about the rest of the letter? Paul appears to have given no indication of his reasons for communicating the substance of 1:16—11:36 to the saints in Rome. Douglas Campbell has recently remarked on the complex structural tensions inherent in the letter: "a practical letter frame oriented primarily toward converted pagans wrapped around a highly abstract, coherent letter body oriented apparently toward Jewish issues."[3] In his view, the substantial contra-Jewish section has been constructed, with great rhetorical ingenuity, for the purpose of forestalling the pending disruptive influence of the "hostile countermissionaries" who have dogged Paul's steps from Jerusalem, through Syrian Antioch, Galatia, Philippi, and now to Rome.[4] For explicit evidence the thesis relies heavily on a brief passage towards the close of the letter (16:17–20) in which Paul warns the Romans to be on the lookout for "those who cause divisions and create obstacles contrary to the doctrine that you have been taught." It is difficult to believe, however, that the whole argument of Romans is to be accounted for by this belated, "caustic," and opaque reference to people who are not, in any case, clearly characterized as "false teachers." They are capable of deceiving the innocent "by smooth talk and flattery," but no connection is made with the major themes of the letter or points of disagreement: they are merely said to serve their own "appetites."

Undoubtedly, in this passage Paul identifies a significant threat to the integrity and obedience of the community in Rome, which may well have been in the back of his mind while composing the letter. But as a primary explanation for the scope and shape of the material, this is much too oblique and in the end too limited. I will suggest later that what is at stake here is not Paul's Law-free gospel as a matter of principle but the willingness of the community—in the language of Romans 8—to be conformed to the image of Christ in his suffering for the sake of the future of the people of God. For now, it seems to me that a much more straightforward, historically plausible explanation is available to us, which is that in 1:16—11:36 Paul rehearses an extended argument regarding the substance, scope, and implications of the "gospel" that he

3. Campbell, *Deliverance of God*, 471.

4. Ibid., 495–518.

intends to proclaim in Rome and then in the western empire. The argument begins with the proclamation that Jesus has been appointed the Son of God in power by his resurrection from the dead (1:4), but that merely sets the cat among the pigeons. The vigorous diatribe-style—the expostulations, the exchanges with fictive interlocutors—is indicative of the fact that this gospel-argument was motivated and shaped in public and often heated debate, in synagogues, homes, marketplaces, and magistrates' courts, from Jerusalem to Illyricum. Ernst Käsemann asks: "do not the many digressions and the leaps in the train of thought show that what we have here is not a self-contained treatise but the deposit of many debates which, because of its conversational character, which shines through everywhere, should be given the title 'Dialogue with the Jews' . . . ?"[5] The striking literary and conceptual familiarity with the texts of Second Temple Judaism that we find in chapters 1–11 in particular is strong evidence that the argument has emerged out of extensive dialogue with—and presupposes the outlook of—the synagogues. If there are traces of the furious engagement with a reactionary Jewish Christianity that we know frustrated Paul's work at many turns, there is no good reason to think that it is directed against specific opponents in Rome. It is again simply part of the argument and of the controversy that it provoked. The fact that Paul makes reference to Jews and *Greeks* specifically suggests that he has in mind his experiences in the eastern, Greek-speaking empire. The "barbarians" to which he refers in 1:14 would have been "unsophisticated" non-Greek-speaking peoples *within*, rather than beyond, the sphere of the *oikoumenē*—the world as it was subject to Greco-Roman culture and rule.

The rhetorical context can be demonstrated from Acts, whatever we may make of the historicity of Luke's work. For example, the eschatological contours of Paul's sermon in the synagogue in Pisidian Antioch can be plotted at numerous points against the argument of Romans 1:16—11:36

---

5. Käsemann, *Romans*, 33–34; "Dialogue with the Jews" is Jeremias's phrase. Cf. Barrett: "It often becomes easier to follow Paul's arguments if the reader imagines the apostle face to face with a heckler, who makes interjections and receives replies which sometimes are withering and brusque. It is by no means impossible that some of the arguments in Romans first took shape in this way, in the course of debates in synagogue or market place" (Barrett, *Romans*, 43). Witherington and Hyatt suggest that Paul is "in a sense impersonating himself as if he were already in Rome . . ." (Witherington and Hyatt, *Romans*, 77).

(Acts 13:16–41). He first tells the story of Israel's formation, culminating in the kingdom under David. God has brought a savior to Israel, a son of David according to the flesh. Before his coming, however, John proclaimed a baptism of repentance to all the people of Israel, convinced that the axe was already laid to the root of the trees, that wrath was coming upon the nation (cf. Matt 3:1–10; Luke 3:3–9). The message of this salvation for Israel has been sent to the Jews and God-fearing Gentiles of the *oikoumenē* because the leaders and citizens of Jerusalem failed to recognize the savior or understand the prophets. They had him killed, but Paul and his companions now bring the good news that God has fulfilled his promises to the fathers by raising Jesus from the dead—as it is written in Psalm 2: "You are my Son, today I have begotten you." Through Jesus the forgiveness of Israel's sins is proclaimed to the Jewish communities of the diaspora. The Law of Moses can only condemn sinful Israel to destruction; but they can be set free from this condemnation by believing the good news that is now proclaimed to them. Paul concludes with a dire warning that is fully in keeping with the tenor of his gospel in Romans. If they do not grasp this salvation, the words of the prophet Habakkuk will come true for them: "Look, you scoffers, be astounded and perish; for I am doing a work in your days, a work that you will not believe, even if one tells it to you." Needless to say, the Jews do not heed the warning, do not believe that judgment is coming on their people, and do not accept the offer of a new life in the age to come. So Paul and Barnabas turn to the Gentiles (Acts 13:44–47).

This does not mean that Paul has not to some degree adapted this exposition of his good news to the circumstances and needs of the community in Rome (cf. 6:11, 17–18; 11:13), or that he does not intersperse commentary and reflection for the benefit of his readers, or even that he successfully sustains the conceit through to the end of chapter 11. But there is precious little to suggest that he has constructed his argument in these chapters in order to answer theological or pastoral controversies that were troubling his readers in Rome. The questions that he addresses in the course of his discourse are those that would have been thrown at him by outraged Jews (and no doubt the occasional Gentile) as they listened to his claim that the God of Israel had transformed the destiny of his people by raising Jesus from the dead and elevating him above even the most potent and dangerous gods of the ancient world: Then what advantage has the Jew? Or what is the value of circumcision? Is God unrighteous to inflict wrath on us? Are we Jews any better off? Are we to continue in sin that grace may abound? Are we to sin because we are not under Law but under grace? Shall we say that the Law is sin? Is there injustice on God's part? Why does he still find fault? For who can resist his will? Has God rejected his people?

We will proceed, therefore, on the basis of the following assumptions. In the first place, the Letter to the Romans is Paul's presentation of himself to the churches in Rome as an apostle to the nations who no longer finds room to work in the eastern empire and is anxious to secure, in some representative form at least, the obedience of the nations across the Western Roman world before it is too late.

Secondly, it provides a consolidated but thorough recapitulation of his gospel-argument concerning the hope of the people of God as it has emerged from innumerable conversations, altercations, debates, and judicial defenses, and no doubt from Paul's reflection on the mixed reception of his message. Contextualizing this material in this way has considerable benefits for interpretation. Apart from its inherent rhetorical plausibility within the framework of Paul's apostolic career, it does away with the need to construct a complex sociological scenario that might make sense of the apparent split between Jewish and Gentile interests in Rome. Romans 1:16—11:36 has the form, primarily, of an engagement with the Jews because both practically and theologically for Paul the task of preaching the gospel to the nations took a headlong route through the dense and thorny thickets of Jewish incomprehension and intransigence. The proclamation of the gospel to the Gentiles was always by way of the controversy with Judaism.

Thirdly, the letter sets out certain aspects of how Paul expected the predominantly Gentile churches in Rome to exist as an authentic and durable "offering of the nations" under the eschatological conditions determined by the gospel-argument. Given the prominence of the theme in the letter, it may well be that in Paul's mind these churches represented more sharply than other congregations the role that the nations would play in the fulfillment of Jewish hopes—a state of affairs to which the expulsion of the Jews from the city by Claudius, probably in AD 49, may well have contributed (Acts 18:2; Suetonius *Claud.* 25.4). They are bracketed with "the rest of the nations" in 1:13 (my translation), and Paul provides as the reason for wanting to "preach the gospel to you also who are in Rome" the fact that he is under obligation both to Greeks and to barbarians, both to the wise and to the foolish, with no mention of the Jews (1:13–14). He interjects an explicit address to "you, the nations" in 11:13 (my translation) and the ensuing parable of the olive tree is clearly meant to correct certain misconceptions entertained by Gentile believers regarding the status of the Jews. Finally, we may observe that Romans 12:1—15:7 is much less reliant on Scripture than the gospel-argument. To some extent this simply reflects the change in content, but it is at least consistent with the view that Paul has in mind a Gentile audience and not the mainly Jewish audience presupposed in 1:16—11:36.[6]

These are not discrete objectives. The gospel-argument accounts both for his apostolic role and for the foreseen eschatological conditions under which the dispersed communities of "saints" must exist. This is clear not least from the summary statement of Romans 15:7–9. The saints in Rome should receive one another as they have been received by the Jewish Christ, who became a servant to Israel for two purposes: to ensure the future of the descendants of Abraham, and to incorporate the nations into the worship of Israel's God. We will see that this account of Jesus's servanthood is an exact and succinct synopsis of the argument that is developed in 1:16—11:36. Whatever other purpose it may serve in representing Paul's apostolic ministry to the saints in Rome, it establishes the grounds for the appeal to the saints in Romans 12:1–2 to present their "bodies as a living sacrifice, holy and acceptable to God, which is your spiritual worship."

The Gospel of God: 1:1–4

Paul introduces himself to his readers as a servant of Christ Jesus, called to be an apostle and set apart for the "gospel of God." This gospel is not to be privatized: it is a public announcement regarding something that will have an impact on nations. It is not less far-reaching than the *euangelion*

---

6. It is this division between a fictive public audience and the actual recipients of the letter that accounts for apparent tensions such as that between a strong anti-Jewish stance in the gospel-argument and attempts to moderate the arrogance of the "strong" Gentile section of the community in Rom 11:17–24 and chapter 14: see, for example, Campbell, *Deliverance of God*, 484–95.

proclaimed to the ruins of Jerusalem and the cities of Judah that the Lord will deliver his people in the sight of the nations, that those who suffer and mourn because of the captivity of Israel will be restored (Isa 40:9; 52:7–10; 61:1–3 LXX; cf. Matt 11:4–5; Luke 4:17–19); nor will it prove to be of any less political significance than the *euangelion* of the great blessings bestowed by Providence on the world that began with the "birthday of the god Augustus."[7] In Paul's mind the gospel of God concerning his Son, physically descended from David, but "determined Son of God in power according to the Spirit of holiness by resurrection from the dead" (1:4, my translation), is a matter of immense historical importance both for Jews and for the people of the world governed by Caesar. This is not to say that this conviction has been constructed, whether by Paul or by some earlier tradition, in self-consciously dissenting opposition to the blasphemous acclamation of Caesar as "son of god"—as a "critical counterpart to the central institution of the Roman Empire" (Georgi).[8] The truculent empire-critical turn that the New Perspective on Paul has recently taken is not altogether convincing. *As far as the argument of Romans goes,* the "obedience of the nations"[9] that Paul is bent on securing means obedience to YHWH—in contrast to the *disobedience* of Israel—not defiance of Caesar. Neil Elliott has to admit that Romans "offers no direct critique of empire," and the argument for an *indirect* critique is undermined by the lack of intertextual reference.[10] Paul clearly engages with the Jewish Scriptures and to a lesser extent with the rhetoric and literature of Hellenistic Judaism, but there is little evidence of a deliberate engagement, subversive or otherwise, with the ideology of Roman imperialism. Nevertheless, the scope and impact of the announcement about the "Son of God" must be registered in political terms.[11] A salient passage from the

---

7. Priene Calendar Inscription; for the translation see Evans, "Mark's Incipit," 68–69. Cf. Wright, *Romans*, 415; Witherington and Hyatt, *Romans*, 31–32.

8. Cited in Elliott, *Arrogance*, 63.

9. Note the debate over the sense of the genitive construction: Dunn, *Romans 1–8*, 17–18; Wright, *Romans*, 420; Witherington and Hyatt, *Romans*, 34–35. If the contrast with disobedient Israel is primary, then the obedience is to be understood as broader than faith or faithfulness but dependent in some way upon it. If the eschatological argument is in view, the obedience of the nations is the faithfulness that will see them through the day of wrath.

10. Elliott, *Arrogance*, 61.

11. Cf. Elliott, *Arrogance*, 62–65.

Psalms and another instance of Paul's preaching in Acts help us to grasp this point.

Kirk is quite right in thinking that the appointment of Jesus as "Son of God in power" has its conceptual origins in Old Testament enthronement theology and in particular in the divine proclamation to Israel's king, whom he has "set on Zion": "You are my Son; today I have begotten you" (Ps 2:6–7).[12] He is mistaken, however, in supposing that the promise implicit in this allusion—that Jesus will be given the nations as an inheritance—points simply to the inclusion of Gentiles in the people of God. What the Psalm has in view, either literally or poetically, is an act of foreign defiance towards YHWH and aggression against his anointed king. YHWH's response is to assure the king that he has *this day* given birth to him as a son, the consequence of which is that the king who is threatened by the nations will receive them as an inheritance, the ends of the earth as a possession—to be broken with a rod of iron, dashed to pieces like a potter's vessel (Ps 2:8–9). The promise, therefore, entailed in the metaphor of *begetting* is that Israel's king will have victory over the nations that oppose him. The Psalm concludes with a warning to the kings of the earth not to conspire against the God of Israel but to fear him, or they risk being destroyed by his wrath. If this story lies behind the argument of Romans 1:4, the thought is not that the Gentiles are being included in the people of God but that the one who has been appointed Son of God in power will eventually conquer and rule over the nations. Elliott has this about right, though he will make too much of the anti-imperial implications: "If God had in fact vindicated Jesus as the one who would 'rise to rule the nations' (Rom 15:12; Isa 11:10), then God's redemption and vindication of Israel against an ungodly empire would soon and inevitably follow."[13]

If we are accustomed to thinking of the gospel in wholly benign and personal terms, this may be a disturbing and incongruous notion. But the potential for interpreting *in terms of future political-religious outcomes* the argument about Christ and the nations—and indeed, the whole argument in Romans about the future confirmation of the righteousness of God—is illustrated by Eusebius's exuberant celebration of the restoration of the churches by Constantine and Licinius in the language of the Psalms

---

12. Kirk, *Unlocking Romans*, 41–42. The explanatory relationship between Jesus's resurrection and Ps 2:7 is also illustrated by Acts 13:33; Heb 5:1–5.

13. Elliott, "Apostle Paul and Empire," 104.

(Eusebius *Hist. eccl.* 10.1.1–7). He sings a new song after the long dark years of persecution, for "The Lord has made known his salvation; he has revealed his righteousness in the sight of the nations" (Ps 98:2). In this turn of events the words of Psalm 46:9 have been "clearly fulfilled": "He makes wars cease to the end of the earth; he breaks the bow and shatters the spear; he burns the chariots with fire." At long last, the "whole race of God's enemies was destroyed . . . and disappeared in a moment" (cf. Ps 37:35–36).

The second passage is Paul's address to the Athenians on the Areopagus, in which he brings his polite—and no doubt politic—critique of pagan worship to an abrupt conclusion by affirming that God "has fixed a day on which he will judge the world (*oikoumenēn*) in righteousness by a man whom he has appointed; and of this he has given assurance to all by raising him from the dead" (Acts 17:31). The same verb is used for "appointed" (*horizō*) as in Romans 1:4; it is an appointment validated by Jesus's resurrection from the dead; and the fact that it is an appointment as judge of an obsolescent political system—the *oikoumenēn*—underlines the relevance of our reading of Psalm 2 for the interpretation of Romans 1:4.[14] We will have more to say on this later, but it is immediately apparent that this sermon has much in common with Paul's argument in the opening chapters of Romans.

Among All the Nations: 1:5

Davina Lopez's book *Apostle to the Conquered* is a good example of what has probably been the most significant turn that Pauline studies have taken following the New Perspective. As an overtly *gender-critical* analysis the book takes a step beyond the empire-critical work of scholars such as John Dominic Crossan, Richard Horsley, and Neil Elliott; but it operates, nevertheless, broadly from a theoretical position that has "rediscovered the Roman Empire as a world to which Paul responds."[15] The New Perspective has properly corrected the Western theological tradition's preoccupation with the spiritual condition of the individual consciousness and—somewhat incidentally—a supposed anti-Jewish bias. But

14. In Acts 10:42 Jesus is "appointed (*hōrismenos*) by God" in more general terms to be "judge of the living and the dead."

15. Lopez, *Apostle*, xii.

insofar as it still thinks of Paul's "self-presentation and rhetoric as exclusively religious and theological," it fails to take adequate account of the broader political questions of Jewish existence in an imperial context.[16] The critique is valid at least in its first part: more clearly in Romans than anywhere else Paul addresses the long-term issue of the political-religious destiny of a distinctive people group struggling to define and preserve its identity under a pagan imperial system. Whether that argument is adequately framed as a confrontation with empire *per se* is another matter.

Lopez takes as her point of departure two classical images, one literary, the other sculptural. The first is taken from Suetonius's account of Nero's mental and political decline: in a dream he is "surrounded by the statues of the nations which had been dedicated in Pompey's theatre and stopped in his tracks" (Suetonius *Nero* 46.1). The second is a relief sculpture from the imperial cult complex in Aphrodisias in Asia Minor, which shows the emperor Claudius subjugating the nation Britannia, depicted as a half-naked woman. Out of these Lopez creates a composite representation of the nations conquered and subsequently effeminized by Roman male power, and then asks what it would mean to examine Paul's rhetoric in the light of this imagery. Paul's "good news" to the nations, she suggests, is that "they no longer are captive and enslaved to a victorious general or raped and killed by divine emperors, but are (re-)born as children of Abraham and belong to the God who brought the Israelites (and others) out of Egypt."[17]

At issue here, in the first place, is the sense that we give to *ta ethnē*— the "Gentiles" or "nations." Within the purview of contemporary New Testament scholarship, Lopez argues, the Gentiles are invariably construed non-sociologically and non-politically as peoples who are *not adherents of the Jewish cult*: "Gentiles do not have a real definition or substance of their own, except in relation to Jews and Israel."[18] Even recent theological perspectives that have affirmed Paul's essential Jewishness fail to consider the independent historical identity of "the nations": "They exist only in an ideal theological other-world, where they are urged to become religious in the right way.

16. Ibid., 122.
17. Ibid., 3.
18. Ibid., 5.

Normally speaking, within the closed symbolic world of the New Testament, images such as the sculptural depiction of Claudius and Britannia are permitted no significant interpretive function; but Lopez asks whether they might "tell us something about how to imagine the real world of the Pauline letters." In opposition to the sort of "rational" biblical scholarship that has generated "an ideal theological world, where there is no real context for Paul's rhetoric besides personal religious piety and struggles over dogmatic correctness," she describes a non-idealist hermeneutic that attempts to re-imagine Paul's relationship with the Gentiles "through an examination of the ideology of conquest and universal domination in the Roman Empire."[19] In other words, she wants to consider how Paul would appear to us if we considered *ta ethnē* in relation not to Jerusalem but to Rome—if we were to suppose that Nero's nightmares about the insubordinate and obstructive nations were, in fact, of central symbolic relevance to Paul's mission.

What she proposes is a "gender-critical re-imagination of Paul as apostle to the defeated nations as part of a non-idealist framework that draws on elements from contemporary empire-critical, postcolonial, feminist, and queer theoretical contributions."[20] By "non-idealist" she means an approach that obliges historical-criticism to take proper account, first, of the concrete social contexts of biblical texts ("including political and economic structures, patterns of domination and subordination, and marginalization") and, secondly, of the "wider variety of cultural artifacts" by which a social context must be described. Moreover—and more urgently—a non-idealist reading is inherently liberationist in that it seeks to detach the Bible from interpretations "aligned with privilege, elitism, and imperialism that masquerade as value-neutral" and which obscure the "gospel of the poor" that is central to both the Old and the New Testaments. The *empire-critical* component is an extension of the non-idealist grounding of the text. The "New Testament is seen as a collection of documents demonstrating negotiation of and resistance to Roman imperial rule."[21] *Postcolonial* analyses make a sharper, but for Lopez ambiguous, contribution. There is a repudiation of modern biblical exegesis as being "thoroughly implicated in the perpetuation of imperialism and

19. Ibid., 6.
20. Ibid., 7.
21. Ibid., 9.

colonialism." But if the further conclusion is reached that the Bible itself endorses an inherently colonial project to dominate the world, "its texts and contradictions are rendered impotent for social transformation from the margins in the present."[22] Finally, *feminist and queer* approaches put forward gender and sexuality as "useful optics for seeing more adequately the hierarchical relations of power operative in the Roman Empire of Paul's time."[23]

In light of these theoretical perspectives, Lopez argues that it is possible to "recontextualize, in a non-idealist way, the Gentiles and nations and position them as occupying the same semantic field as the poor and marginalized." Paul then appears as apostle to the marginalized and the defeated, which connects with the "preferential option for the poor and marginalized at the core of the Bible."[24] Within a Jewish framework the Gentiles are those peoples who are not Israel, and Paul's mission appears as a struggle to "build different relationships," subsuming both Jews and Gentiles under a common ancestor determined by his "trust" in God. Within the framework of the Roman "imaginary" or ideology, however, the fate of *ta ethnē* is to be "found, conquered, and incorporated into the Roman family through military violence and diplomacy, as well as subsequent enslavement and death." From this perspective Israel is simply one among the many nations that have been subjugated by Roman military power.[25] Indeed, Josephus has Agrippa warn the Jews that if they persist in their determination to go to war, the Romans will burn Jerusalem and destroy the nation in order to make of them "an example to the rest of the nations" (Josephus *J. W.* 2.397, LCL). In its apocalyptic resistance to empire Israel constitutes an outstanding instance of nationhood defined in relation to Rome. Lopez believes that the Jewish definition of the "Gentiles," drawn from the Septuagint usage, remains influential for Paul's mission, but argues that in the process a re-mapping occurs so that in the end the good news that Paul proclaims to the nations may be construed from a quite different perspective: it is that the nations may be liberated from their enslavement to violent, exploitative imperialism through an alliance

---

22. Ibid., 10.

23. Ibid., 15.

24. Ibid., 22.

25. Ibid., 110–13.

with liberated Israel on the basis of trust in God and inclusion in the multi-national family of Abraham.

It is an impressive and engaging thesis, but is there any evidence that the term is re-mapped in Paul to the extent that he understood himself as apostle to the nations *as Rome's other* rather than *as Israel's other*? Lopez puts forward two broad arguments. The first amounts to little more than a non-idealist inference: Paul was so exposed to and so fluent in the pervasive visual and literary narratives of Roman hegemony (described in detail in chapters 2 and 3) that he was bound to have assimilated the reversed perspective on the nations that they entailed. The second argument has a more exegetical character. Lopez suggests that Paul's conversion consisted of a radical shift of consciousness from violent persecutor to conquered Jew, from dominator to dominated, from "impenetrable masculinity to penetrable femininity," and in that respect mirrored the relationship between Rome and the nations.[26] "What Paul is forced to come to heightened consciousness about is that to the Romans, the nations include the Jews—and they all are persecuted ravaged, and re-created, by a larger force. God reveals to Paul that he has Christ 'in him,' that he has the dynamics of defeat by the Romans within him."[27]

How well does this work? The singular *ethnos* denotes a "nation" or "people"—never an individual "Gentile" as such. In the New Testament, however, it does not always work in English to translate the plural *ethnē* as "nations." For example, Luke writes that following the preaching of Paul and Barnabas in the synagogue at Iconium "a great number of Jews and Greeks believed," but then "unbelieving Jews stirred up and poisoned the souls of *tōn ethnōn* against the brothers" (my translation). Later an attempt is made by both *tōn ethnōn* and the Jews, along with their rulers, to insult them and stone them (Acts 14:1–5). In this context *ta ethnē* clearly refers not to the nations at a distance but to numbers of individuals who are not Jews; the term is virtually synonymous with "Greeks." Presumably when Paul tells the pagan citizens of Lystra that in previous generations God "allowed *panta ta ethnē* to walk in their own ways," he is thinking of the nations as peoples who have not known the one true God, who had revealed himself explicitly to the Jews (Acts 14:16). The "Gentiles" are people or peoples, whether conceived abstractly or encountered con-

---

26. Ibid., 124–37.

27. Ibid., 135.

cretely, who derive their identity from their non-Israelite nationality. It is easy enough to demonstrate that Paul's usage does not break out of this pattern, even if it may be entirely appropriate in many instances to translate *ta ethnē* as "the nations," with full awareness of the political resonances generated within the Greco-Roman *oikoumenē*.

The frequent use of the term in the New Testament, however, also presupposes two closely linked story-lines, both rooted in the Jewish Scriptures, which are really determinative for meaning. The first views the nations as aggressive powers that oppose Israel, both religiously and politically; they are likely at some point to destroy Jerusalem and defile its sanctuary as a manifestation of God's anger against his people; but there is always the prospect of an eventual victory over the nations and the establishment of the Jews as a preeminent people. At this point the second story-line is engaged: when YHWH intervenes decisively to judge and restore his people, messengers are sent to proclaim news of the event to the nations, which may lead to the participation of the nations in the worship of Israel's God, potentially in fulfillment of the promise to Abraham that he would be the father of, and a blessing to, many nations.

The first of these stories provides a framework for understanding Jesus's suffering: his crucifixion by an imperial power anticipates the mass crucifixion of Jews by Rome during the course of the war and becomes, therefore, symbolic of Israel's punishment. Paul certainly identifies with this suffering, and he urges the communities to which he writes to participate in the same narrative of death and vindication. At this point, it seems to me, Lopez's empire-critical argument—and to a lesser extent the gender-critical spin that she puts on it—offers credible and intriguing insight into the political-religious character of Paul's very deliberate association with a crucified messiah.

However, Paul then assimilates the suffering into the second narrative, which is explanatory of his own calling: he is the messenger to the nations who is subjected to physical abuse by both Jews and non-Jews—indeed, it is precisely this persecution that validates his apostleship. He suffers not on behalf of the nations brutalized by Rome but on behalf of Christ implicated in Israel's punishment. In this narrative the fact of oppression as a general political evil is not negated, but it is subordinated to the overriding issue of Israel's salvation—that is, a salvation concretely and politically, and therefore not merely religiously and theologically, conceived as a matter of the ongoing integrity and survival of the community.

There is no moment in Paul's narratively constructed self-understanding, therefore, that permits or requires the sort of re-mapping of the "nations" that Lopez is arguing for. The distinction that she makes between a rhetoric of personal piety and a rhetoric of anti-imperial struggle is too crude. We may well think that Paul is fully aware of the theo-political implications of his gospel and the concrete, non-idealist existence of the communities that he addresses; but this does not necessarily mean that he understood himself as apostle to the nations subjugated by Rome rather than to the nations that "worshipped and served the creature rather than the Creator" (Rom 1:25) or that raged and conspired against YHWH and his anointed king (Ps 2:1–3). The end point for Paul, as is clear not least from his Letter to the Romans, is deliverance not from Rome but from the wrath of God. What follows *that* story, however, is another matter.

3

Beginning (Unfortunately) with the Wrath of God

The good news came because Gods wrath is approaching

Paul unashamedly pursues his calling to make known to the Greco-Roman world that the God of the Jews has raised Jesus from the dead, appointing him to a position of authority over the nations. Having stated his intention to proclaim this good news also to the community of saints in Rome, he sets out in programmatic fashion the grounds for his confidence.[1] His *gospel* is the power of God for *salvation* for all who believe it—both for the Jew, in the first place, and for the Greek (1:16). It is effective for salvation because in it the *righteousness* of God is revealed. A terse aphorism from the prophet Habakkuk establishes a connection between the theme of righteousness and the personal response of *faith(fulness)* (1:17)—the cumbersome locution is a placeholder for a postponed consideration of how best to translate the word *pistis*. The aphorism is linked directly to the contention that the *wrath* of God is "revealed from heaven against all ungodliness and unrighteousness of men, who by their unrighteousness suppress the truth" (1:18), which elicits what must be for now a final explanatory clause: for "what can be known about God is plain to them, because God has shown it to them" (1:19). This brings us to the end of the juddering plank from which we must leap into the murky and swirling depths of Paul's public argument about the gospel of God.

---

1. There is a tendency amongst commentators to regard only 1:16–17 as the *propositio*, reflecting a general inclination to marginalize the theme of wrath (e.g., Witherington and Hyatt, *Romans*, 47–57). The quotation from Habakkuk, however, presupposes judgment, first on Israel, then on the Chaldeans, which makes it appropriate to include the statement about the revelation of the wrath of God in the *propositio*.

It is immediately apparent that the five terms highlighted here—gospel, salvation, righteousness, faith(fulness), and wrath—fix the coordinates for a good part, if not all, of Paul's comprehensive reworking of his thesis in Romans 1:16—11:36. But it is important to note that while the rhetoric sets out from "gospel" and proceeds in the direction of "wrath," the theological reasoning travels purposefully in the opposite direction: it is *because* (*gar*) the wrath of God is revealed against unrighteousness that Habakkuk's statement about the righteous living by faith(fulness) acquires eschatological prominence; the aphorism then tells us something about the revelation of the righteousness of God, which is the reason why (*gar*) salvation has become available to everyone who believes, the Jew first, then the Gentile; and then finally it is the "power" of this salvation that accounts for (*gar*) Paul's confidence in preaching to the nations the gospel of Jesus's extraordinary accession. Or to put it more concisely: Paul unashamedly proclaims the good news about the resurrected son of God because . . . because . . . because . . . because the day of God's wrath against both Jews and Greeks is approaching.[2]

So we must begin where Paul begins the lengthy exposition of his gospel in Romans, with the revelation of the "wrath of God" as the foundational premise of his argument. We need to consider where this thought comes from, how it is likely to have been understood in the specific context of his mission to the nations, and what part it plays in the emerging argument of the letter. Paul gives considerable space (1:18—2:16) to a theme that has a widespread, complex, and powerful background in Jewish thought. If we proceed in too much of a hurry—perhaps because we find the whole subject of divine wrath outmoded or even unconscionable—it is likely that we will become disoriented and head off in entirely the wrong direction.

The Wrath of God Is Revealed from Heaven: 1:18

God's wrath is coming from Heaven

For the most part in Romans the phrase has in view a *future event*—a "day of wrath when God's righteous judgment will be revealed" (2:5), when he

2. Cf. Elliott, *Arrogance*, 74; Dunn, *Romans 1–8*, 70, thinks that the *gar* of 1:18 may "demonstrate that wrath is the presupposition of or preliminary to righteousness—the need for and nature of God's righteousness can be understood only when we have first understood the outworking of divine wrath"; but he does not commit himself to a strong causal connection.

will "render to each according to his works" (2:6), when he will judge the secrets of people's hearts (2:16), an outcome from which those who have been "justified" by Jesus's death will be saved (5:9), a day when a God of "vengeance" (*ekdikēsis*) will repay those who do evil against his people (12:19). Paul's argument about wrath, however, begins not in the future but in the present: "the wrath of God *is revealed* from heaven against all ungodliness and unrighteousness of men" (1:18). What does he mean by this *present* revelation of wrath, how has it been made known, and how does it relate to the future day of wrath?

The *present revelation* (*apokalyptetai*) of the wrath of God from heaven clearly stands parallel to the *present revelation* (*apokalyptetai*) of the righteousness of God in the gospel. This affords us with an immediate reference point for interpretation. Wright argues from the general structure of Paul's apocalyptic thought that the wrath of God has been "split into two": it is still to be revealed in the future, but "the last day has in some sense been brought forward into the present."[3] Since the moral corruption of the pagan world cannot be said to constitute a novel or "fresh" revelation of the wrath of God, Paul must mean that in some way "the fact of Jesus has drawn back the veil on the wrath to come." The explanation for this lies in the appointment of Jesus as judge of the whole world, which is the content of Paul's gospel (cf. Rom 2:16; Acts 17:31). Both the righteousness and the wrath of God, therefore, are disclosed in the same way—that is, through the gospel.

However, while it is true that the future *day* of wrath will be a day on which God will judge the pagan world through Jesus Christ, we are not bound to conclude from the supposed split structure of Paul's eschatology that the foreshadowing or disclosure of God's wrath through events or circumstances other than the gospel is ruled out—and there are good reasons to think that Paul has something other than the gospel in mind here. First, if the phrase "from heaven" is not to be regarded as redundant, merely a reinforcement of the *tou theou*, it suggests both a contrast with the revelation of the righteousness of God *in the gospel* (*en autō*) and a more direct mode of disclosure.[4] Secondly, the present tense does not necessarily imply a novel or recent revelation: it may signify a

---

3. Wright, *Romans*, 431.

4. Cf. Fitzmyer, *Romans*, 277: "The prep. phrase *ap' ouranou*, 'from heaven,' i.e., from God, has to be understood as contrasted with *en autō*, 'in it,' i.e., in the gospel (v 17)."

general state of affairs, much as Paul argues in v. 19 that "what can be known about God is plain to them" from the nature of things. Thirdly, the language of v. 18 does not look backwards in the passage—there is no mention of Jesus, gospel, resurrection, or judgment. Rather it anticipates the argument of 1:19–32 that God has handed over the "godless," those who suppress the truth, to "unrighteousness," the final outcome of which is death. This suggests that the wrath of God is revealed not in the announcement about Jesus but in a pre-history to the day of wrath. We find this immediately in the argument about the disastrous consequences of idolatry in 1:19–32; but it is also consistent with, and arguably shaped by, the story about righteousness and *pistis* in Habakkuk. Both these stories need to be told.

The Argument against Paganism: 1:19–32

The view is quite widely accepted by commentators that it is in the story of human degradation told in 1:19–32 that the wrath of God is—from Paul's perspective—presently revealed.[5] The pagan world has suppressed any true knowledge of God and has made the mother of all category mistakes in exchanging the glory of the Creator, whose "eternal power and divine nature" should have been evident in the "things that have been made," for images of created things. The wrath of God is then understood to be revealed in the story of God *handing over* idolatrous humanity, first, to uncleanness and the dishonoring of their bodies; secondly, to dishonorable passions and same-sex relations; and thirdly, to "a debased mind to do what ought not to be done." In other words, the spiritual and moral condition of the pagan world provides observable evidence of God's displeasure.

In the Septuagint the verb *paradidōmi* is often used to speak of people being delivered by God into the hands of their enemies (e.g., Deut 21:10; Ps 40:3; Ezek 39:23; Dan 3:32), which is enough to explain how the simple fact of *handing over* could amount to an expression of divine judg-

---

5. Käsemann, *Romans*, 38 puts it succinctly: "according to the context immorality is the punishment, not the guilt." Cf. Dunn, *Romans 1–8*, 70: "wrath not as God's final judgment, but as God's response to and indeed part in the unfolding of events and relationships at both personal and corporate level"; Witherington and Hyatt, *Romans*, 65; Elliott, *Arrogance*, 77.

ment. We have stronger precedents for Paul's metaphorical usage in Ben Sirach: Wisdom will abandon the man who goes astray and will "hand him over (*paradōsei*) into the hands of his fall" (Sir 4:19, my translation); and Ben Sirach prays, "Let not the belly's appetite and sexual intercourse seize me, and do not give me over (*paradōis*) to a shameless soul" (Sir 23:6).[6] The more significant literary background, however, is to be found in Psalm 80:9–13 LXX (= Ps 81:8–12), which describes the blatant rebelliousness of the exodus generation. The people of Israel disregarded the command not to worship foreign gods, so God "sent (*exapesteila*) them in the stubbornness of their heart to walk in their own counsels" (my translation). If we read this Psalm in conjunction with Psalm 106, which was clearly also in Paul's mind, we see how serious—indeed, deadly— the consequences were for an elect subset of humankind that had the temerity to exchange "the glory of God for the image of an ox that eats grass" (Ps 106:20). Because they adopted the religious practices of the nations, became subject to their carved images, and sacrificed their sons and daughters to the idols of Canaan, the Lord "became furiously angry (*ōrgisthē thymō*) with his people . . . , and he gave (*paredōken*) them into the hands of the nations, and those who hated them ruled over them" (Ps 105:40–41 LXX = Ps 106:40–41).

That Paul uses stories about Israel's disobedience to construct an argument against paganism alerts us to the complex rhetorical function of the passage. We have a palimpsest: an ostensible critique of pagan idolatry written over an imperfectly erased critique of Jewish idolatry. The narrative layering anticipates, on the one hand, the assertion that the inevitable day of wrath will come upon all people, the Jew first, and then the Greek (Rom 2:9), and on the other, the principal indictment that Paul will make against Israel, which is that in the final analysis the Jews are no better than the rest of humanity. In other respects the polemic is a mongrel. There is an opening concession to Stoic thought in the argument that the invisible attributes of God, "namely, his eternal power and divine nature, have been clearly perceived, ever since the creation of the world, in the things that have been made" (1:20). It is likely, however, that the formula-

6. These are stronger parallels than the allusions in Pss 78:29 and 106:14–15 to Num 11:31–35 cited in Dunn, *Romans*, 62. Note also 2 Macc 1:17: "Blessed in every way be our God, who has delivered up (*paredōken*) those who have behaved impiously (*asebēsantas*)"; and Acts 7:42: "God turned away and gave them over (*paredōken autous*) to worship the host of heaven."

tion comes to Paul by way of a developed Hellenistic Jewish response to its pagan environment; and there is no question that in its overall shape Paul's argument reproduces a well-established tradition of polemic against idolatry, represented notably by the sustained diatribe of Wisdom 12–15. This passage is worth giving some consideration to because it is so clearly constitutive of the thought-world within which Paul's argument about the significance of his gospel has taken shape.

The writer takes it as evidence of the righteousness of God that he reproves "little by little those who fall into error" (Wis 12:2), by way of a warning, so that they may have an opportunity to repent. He gives as an example—dubious in more ways than one—the fact that God did not wipe out the ancient Canaanites at a stroke, despite their detestable pagan practices, but "sent wasps as forerunners of your army in order to destroy them little by little" (12:8). In view of this, no one can accuse God of injustice: "For neither is there any god beside you, whose care is for all, to whom you must prove that you did not act unjustly, nor can any king or prince look you in the face concerning those whom you have punished" (12:13–14). All people were foolish by nature, being ignorant of God: they failed to recognize "the one who is" from the good things that are seen, the craftsman from his works, and concluded instead that the world is governed by gods of the elements or of the stars (13:1–2). The writer has some sympathy for those who were seduced by the beauty of created things, though they are still not to be pardoned (13:9); but he has nothing but classic Jewish disdain for those who "designated as gods the work of human hands, gold and silver fashioned with skill, and representations of animals or useless stone, the work of an ancient hand" (13:10).

Both the impious and the impiety, the idolaters and the idols, are hateful to God and will be punished. So there will be a "visitation also upon the idols of the nations, because, though part of the divine creation, they have become an abomination, a stumbling-block for the lives of human beings and a trap for the feet of the foolish" (14:11). For the "invention of idols was the beginning of fornication, and the discovery of them the corruption of life"; they did not exist from the beginning, nor will they last forever; they "entered the world through human conceit, and for this reason their exact purpose was planned (or 'their speedy end was planned')" (14:12–14, my translation). The assumption here is that, for all its devastating impact on humanity, the idolatry that the Jews encountered in the ancient world was an impermanent phase of human history: it had a beginning, and its end has been determined by the God of Israel.

The evil of idolatry reveals itself principally in two practices: the ritual murder of children and the defilement of marriage that attends the "secret mysteries" and "frenzied revels" (14:23–24). But from these erupts "an overwhelming confusion of blood and murder, theft and deceit, corruption, unfaithfulness, tumult, perjury, turmoil of those who are good, forgetfulness of favors, defilement of souls, sexual perversion, disorder in marriages, adultery and debauchery" (14:25–26). So it can be said that the worship of idols is the "beginning and cause and end of every evil" (14:27).

Behind the fulminations of Hellenistic Judaism are Old Testament denunciations of the idolatry of the nations. Jeremiah 10 is especially relevant (cf. Isa 44:6–20). Israel is warned not to learn the "way of the nations" because their superstitions are false and their idols impotent (10:1–5). YHWH is the Creator, who "established the world by his wisdom." Every person was foolish, without knowledge; the images they worship are "a work of delusion" and "at the time of their punishment they shall perish" (10:15); the gods "who did not make the heavens and the earth shall perish from the earth and from under the heavens" (10:11). The passage concludes with an impassioned entreaty: "Pour out your wrath on the nations that know you not, and on the peoples that call not on your name, for they have devoured Jacob; they have devoured him and consumed him, and have laid waste his habitation" (10:25).

Neil Elliott has recently argued, in a highly entertaining and tendentious reading of Romans as a sustained critique of empire, that Paul's analysis of ungodliness and unrighteousness in 1:19–32 has in view neither a universal condition nor the particular disloyalty of the Jews but the appalling shenanigans of the imperial household: "Instead of imputing to Paul a heated, irrational exaggeration as he describes general human sinfulness or an equally stereotyped Judean prejudice regarding the rampant idolatry and immorality of the non-Judean world, we can read every phrase in this passage as an accurate catalog of misdeeds of one or another recent member of the Julio-Claudian dynasty."[7] It is one thing to suggest, of course, that the churches in Rome may have heard in Paul's argument allusions to the depraved behavior of the Caesars or that the pas-

7. Elliott, *Arrogance*, 82.

sage comes splendidly to life when read in conjunction with Suetonius's *Lives of the Caesars*—he writes, for example, of Caligula's "unnatural relations" (*mutui stupri*) with men (Suetonius *Cal.* 36.1). It is another thing to maintain that this constitutes the basic rhetorical intention of this opening section—Paul's analysis is simply too dependent on generic Jewish antecedents for that to be plausible. Nevertheless, Elliott has highlighted the potential that exists for reading it within certain cultural and historical parameters as an argument directed specifically against a system of pagan thought—one which, incidentally, had the capacity to sustain the flagrant blasphemies of the Caesars. The affinity that Romans has with the Wisdom of Solomon underlines the broader polemical focus: a clash of cultures that will culminate in the historical triumph of the singular just God of Israel over the manifold reprobate gods of the nations.

The Revelation of the Wrath of God in Habakkuk

The significance of Habakkuk's narrative for understanding the present revelation of the wrath of God has not generally been recognized. The tightly constructed argument of Romans 1:1–19, however, connects the statement about righteousness and faith(fulness) both with the revelation of the righteousness of God "from faith(fulness) to faith(fulness)" and with the ensuing statement about the revelation of wrath. In fact, we only need to survey the bleak apocalyptic landscape in which the solitary, hopeful tree of Habakkuk's aphorism stands to see how broadly relevant this text is for Paul's argument.

The work begins with the sharp complaint: Why does God not do something about the injustice and violence with which Habakkuk is confronted in Israel? The Law is ineffectual, justice is never done: "the wicked surround the righteous; so justice goes forth perverted" (Hab 1:4). How long will this miserable state of affairs continue? The theme of the prophecy, therefore, is the justification or vindication or righteousness of God.

The response comes abruptly. Habakkuk is told to look for the answer among the nations. God is "raising up the Chaldeans, that bitter and hasty nation, who march through the breadth of the earth, to seize dwellings not their own" (1:6). They have been ordained as a judgment, established for a reproof (1:12): the Babylonian invasion will be the means by which YHWH will punish those in Israel who oppress the righteous, and in this way he will establish his own righteousness. But this terrifying vision only provokes a second complaint: Why does the God of Israel remain silent when the wicked tyrant "swallows up the man more righteous than he" (1:13)? Why is he allowed to trawl through humanity with impunity, as a fisherman trawls through the sea and rejoices over the fish that he amasses? Will Nebuchadnezzar, and others like him, be allowed to keep on emptying the net and "mercilessly killing nations forever" (Hab 1:17)? It is one thing for the unrighteous in Israel to be punished in this way; but what about the righteous?

This time Habakkuk is told to write the answer on tablets so that "he that reads it may run"—may flee from impending calamity, much as Jesus instructed his followers in Judea to flee to the mountains once it was clear that Jerusalem had fallen into enemy hands (Matt 24:15–16; cf. Mark 13:14; Luke 21:20–21). It is only a matter of time: "If it seems slow, wait for it; it will surely come; it will not delay" (2:3). The soul of the tyrant is "puffed up," it is not upright; but in that day of wrath (cf. 2:15; 3:2, 8) the righteous person will live by his faith(fulness) (*be 'emunat/ek pisteōs*).[8]

We find an apposite parallel to this argument in Psalm 31—apposite not least because the line from v. 5, "Into your hand I commit my spirit," is quoted by both Jesus and Stephen exactly at the moment when the hostility of the wicked demands an extreme trust (Luke 23:46; Acts 7:59). The psalmist praises the God who acts in his righteousness to deliver him, who releases him from the net that his enemies have hidden for him; he hates those who "pay regard to worthless idols" and puts his trust instead in God. He prays that those who "speak insolently against the righteous in pride and contempt" will be silenced. God has demonstrated his steadfast love towards him when he was in a besieged city. The Lord "preserves the faithful (*'emunim*) but abundantly repays the one who acts in pride"; so those who "wait for the Lord" should take courage (Ps 31:23–24).

In Habakkuk's narrative, as in Psalm 31, God preserves the person who has faith(fulness) but repays the one who acts in pride—the arrogant man whose appetite for conquest is never satisfied, who "gathers for

---

8. The Hebrew text of Habakkuk 2:4 has "the righteous person by his faithfulness lives"; LXX has "the righteous person by my faithfulness will live." We should assume that "by his/my faithfulness" qualifies "lives / will live" rather than "the righteous person." Habakkuk is concerned about the fate of those who do not commit violence and injustice (cf. 1:3–4). They are righteous because of their behavior, but what will save them from destruction on the day of wrath will be "faithfulness" or trust.

himself all nations and collects as his own all peoples" (Hab 2:5). Sooner or later the tables will be turned: "Because you have plundered many nations, all the remnant of the peoples shall plunder you, for the blood of man and violence to the earth, to cities and all who dwell in them" (Hab 2:8; cf. Isa 10:5–19; 36:13–20). The acquisitive Chaldeans have brought shame upon their house "by cutting off many peoples"; they have forfeited their lives; the stones of the walls and the wooden beams cry out against them (2:9–11). They build cities on foundations of violence and injustice, but "the earth will be filled with the knowledge of the glory of the Lord as the waters cover the sea" (2:12–14). They have forced their neighbors to drink the cup of their wrath, but the "cup in the Lord's right hand will come round to you, and utter shame will come upon your glory!" (2:16). They put their trust in idols that cannot speak or teach and have no breath in them, but "the Lord is in his holy temple; let all the earth keep silence before him" (2:18–20). This is the means by which the justice or righteousness of God is established in the world—not at the terminus of history but where it matters, in the tumultuous course of things, not absolutely but decisively nonetheless with respect to the Chaldeans. Habakkuk quietly waits "for the day of trouble to come upon people who invade us" (3:16).[9]

The Qumran sectarians also found in Habakkuk's prophecy grounds for hope that a community of the righteous would survive when God sent a powerful foreign nation to devastate the land. God has appointed the Kittim (that is, the Romans) for judgment and rebuke, but those who have been chosen because they have observed the commandments will not die: indeed, the tables will be turned and they will be given power to judge the Gentiles (1QpHab 5.1–4; cf. Hab 1:12). Habakkuk 2:4 is interpreted to mean that God will rescue Torah-observant Jews "from among those doomed to judgment, because of their suffering and their loyalty to the Teacher of Righteousness" (1QpHab 8.1–3).

When Paul asserts in Romans 1:18, therefore, that "the wrath of God is revealed from heaven against *all* ungodliness and unrighteousness of men, who by their unrighteousness suppress the truth," he is effectively restating in condensed form the argument of Habakkuk, to whom it was revealed from heaven that not only ungodly and unrighteous Israel but

---

9. LXX reads: "I will rest on a day of affliction to go up to a people of my sojourning."

also the ungodly, unrighteous, and considerably more powerful pagan aggressor would sooner or later be subjected to the wrath of God.[10] Paul understands as well as Habakkuk that a day of wrath entails a risk of serious collateral damage: the forces of oppression and destruction cannot be relied on to discriminate fairly between the guilty and the innocent. How, then, will the righteous survive? They will survive by virtue of their "faith(fulness)"—their 'emuna, their *pistis*.

This "survival" is what Paul means by "salvation to everyone who believes, to the Jew first and also to the Greek" (Rom 1:16). It is a salvation from the wrath of God (cf. 5:9). In light of Habakkuk's argument, we can also see how this salvation needs to be correlated with the revelation of the righteousness of God. God is morally bound to judge the wicked, but he is also morally bound, in Habakkuk's view, to safeguard the righteous: "You who are of purer eyes than to see evil and cannot look at wrong, why do you idly look at traitors and remain silent when the wicked swallows up the man more righteous than he?" (Hab 1:13). When God eventually acts through the contingencies of history to put things right—repaying the arrogant, on the one hand, preserving the faithful, on the other—he is vindicated, he is shown to be righteous. The righteousness of God is determined and disclosed in the action that he takes in order to answer the allegations and complaints—such as Habakkuk's—that are made against him. Whether or not it makes sense to say, as Piper does in his dispute with Wright, that "righteousness of God" denotes an essential quality that is more fundamental than either "God's covenant faithfulness or his impartiality in court," Paul's argument in Romans cannot be made to work at such an abstract level.[11]

Habakkuk's aphorism, however, is not itself the gospel. Paul's good news is not that when the day of wrath comes, the righteous will live by their faithfulness—or in its attenuated modern form, that a person is saved by believing in Jesus. It is that God has raised his Son Jesus from the dead and has given him authority over the nations. This announcement is the "power of God for salvation," and in it the "righteousness of God is

---

10. Wright draws attention to the context of Hab 2:4 but he interprets the wrath as either death or a final judgment (Wright, *Romans*, 425–26, 431, 432). He argues in Wright, *Justification*, 157–58, that "Paul is aware of the entire context in Habakkuk," but he fails to grasp the full paradigmatic potential of such "great crises of Israel's past" for accounting for Paul's argument in Romans.

11. Piper, *Future*, 164.

revealed." What establishes the connection between the "gospel of God" and Habakkuk's crucial insight is the unobtrusive and seemingly pleonastic phrase "from faith(fulness) for faith(fulness)" (*ek pisteōs eis pistin*). It is on the basis of the faithfulness of Jesus, who remained obedient even in the face of death and who was raised from the dead, that others may now have the confidence—may *believe*—that they will not be swept away in the impending flood and storm of God's wrath against ungodliness and unrighteousness but will survive and will find life.

The relevance of this realistic historical context is underlined by the important argument of Hebrews 10:32–39. Fearing that his readers are in danger of falling away (Heb 2:1; 3:12; 6:4–6), the writer reminds them of the "former days when, after you were enlightened, you endured a hard struggle with sufferings, sometimes being publicly exposed to reproach and affliction, and sometimes being partners with those so treated." This suffering, however, is not merely a thing of the past. They are urged in chapter 12 to reflect on Jesus who "endured from sinners such hostility against himself." This should be the inspiration for their own endurance. They have their own struggle against (*antagōnizomenoi*) sin—that is, against the hostility of sinners directed against them: the tyrant Antiochus is said to be the antagonist (*antēgōnizeto*) of the martyrs (4 Macc 17:14). But they "have not yet resisted to the point of shedding your blood" (Heb 12:3–4). If they are indeed, therefore, to gain the promised "better possession" (10:34), the "city that is to come" that will replace devastated Jerusalem (13:14), they will need the sort of endurance that is denoted by Habakkuk's saying about faithfulness. Habakkuk 2:3 has been modified, probably in order to insert Jesus as the "coming" judge who will bring the day of God's wrath. When this occurs, "my righteous one shall live by faith, and if he shrinks back, my soul has no pleasure in him" (Heb 10:38). The writer, therefore, applies Habakkuk's argument to a community that he fears will indeed "shrink back" and be destroyed when the day of God's wrath comes: the stance required has been pioneered and perfected by Jesus, "who for the joy that was set before him endured the cross, despising the shame, and is seated at the right hand of the throne of God" (12:2), but it must be enacted under real eschatological (not mythological) conditions by the community.

4

The Future Day of Wrath

The Righteous Judgment of God: 2:1-11

Paul now directly addresses an audience, and we begin to hear a pugnacious public voice: "Therefore you have no excuse, O man, every one of you who judges (*pas ho krinōn*)" (2:1). There is an intriguing echo here of the opening exhortation of Wisdom of Solomon: "Love righteousness, you who judge the earth (*hoi krinontes tēn gēn*); think about the Lord in goodness, and seek him with sincerity of heart" (Wis 1:1). The kings and "judges (*dikastai*) of the ends of the earth" have received their power from the Most High, and they will be held accountable, not least for the way they have mistreated the righteous of Israel: "Terribly and swiftly he will come upon you, because a severe judgment falls on those in high places" (Wis 6:1–5). Paul also asks whether the one who judges others thinks that he will escape the judgment of God (Rom 2:3); and since he clearly has both the Jew and the Gentile in view here, we might wonder whether he does not pursue his denunciation of moral hypocrisy in a similar vein. Such a sharp political focus, however, cannot be sustained exegetically. The resonance retains some rhetorical force, locating Paul's diatribe in the boisterous arena of Hellenistic-Jewish debate; but chapter 2 appears to have a much more generalized target: "tribulation and distress for every human being who does evil . . . glory and honor and peace for everyone who does good" (2:9).

Moreover, although Paul's language remains frustratingly ambiguous, the argument appears to work best at this juncture if we suppose that the one judging is a Jew, who is challenged, in effect, to consider his own situation *in the light of* the impending judgment of the nations.[1] The account of the degeneration of Greek culture in 1:19–32 does not leave much room at this point for a pagan "judge" in any capacity who stands aloof from the process and condemns others. Paul will shortly acknowledge the existence of righteous non-Jews who are doers of the Law in practice (2:14), but the argument has no need of further grounds for condemning the nations. In addition, there is a knowledge of God and a level of accountability assumed that strongly suggests that this is an argument directed against the Jew;[2] the vocative "O man" has a universal ring to it, but it is used in Romans 9:20 unambiguously to address the Jew who answers back to God;[3] and the simplest way to account for the abrupt shift of focus from the unrighteous person who *approves* of others who do the same things (1:32) to the unrighteous person who *disapproves* of others who do the same things (2:1) is to assume that Paul has switched his attention from the complicit Gentile to the complacent Jew.

The Jew agrees with him that those who worship non-gods have been handed over to depravity as a sign of God's wrath towards them. He agrees that they are, therefore, worthy of death. Indeed, it may even be that, believing himself to be a "guide to the blind, a light to those who are in darkness," he has in one way or another made known this "decree of God" to the nations (1:32; 2:19). But if that is the case, he is without excuse if he then proceeds to do the same things. We Jews certainly know, Paul argues with him, that the "judgment of God rightly falls on those who practice such things" (2:2), but what makes you think that we ourselves are *above the Law*? The Jews in their synagogues have been quick

---

1. Fitzmyer, *Romans*, 299; Dunn, *Romans 1–8*, 79–80; Wright, *Romans*, 438. Elliott disagrees, arguing that "Paul is here indicting the attitude of hypocrisy, not of moral judgment as such (which Protestant scholarship has been too quick to attribute to the 'self-righteous Jew')" (Elliott, *Arrogance*, 83–85).

2. The language of Rom 2:2–10 is especially descriptive of Israel; the word used for hardness of heart (*sklērotēta*) in 2:5 is used of sinful Israel in Deut 9:27.

3. The "reproachful vocative" (Dunn, *Romans 1–8*, 79) is characteristic of the diatribe style (Stowers, *Diatribe*, 85–93), but a similar figure is found in Mic 6:8, which belongs to a prophecy of judgment against the rulers of the house of Israel, who pervert the course of justice and "were passing judgment (*ekrinon*) for a bribe," against the priests who "teach for a price," against the prophets who "practice divination for money" (3:9–11 LXX, my translation), and against those who have acquired wealth through deceit and violence (6:10–15).

to point out that the nations—the misguided and occasionally malevolent *other*—will be punished. Wisdom of Solomon is precisely an admonition to the rulers of the nations that by their idolatry, immorality, injustice, hedonism, and oppression of the righteous they are bringing destruction upon themselves (cf. Wis 1:12; 14:8–14). But, as Paul will argue later, if God is to judge the world on the basis of his decree, he must *first* hold the people of the Law accountable. As long as the Jew persists in emulating the lawless behavior of the nations, he is "storing up wrath" for himself "on the day of wrath when God's righteous judgment will be revealed" (2:5). There will be no judgment of the nations without *first* a judgment of the Jews; there will be no justification of the nations without *first* a justification of the Jews. The insistence that there is no partiality with God (2:11) is aimed at the Jew who thinks that God will punish the sins of the nations and continue to overlook the sins of Israel.

Judgment will come in the form of a "day of wrath when God's righteous judgment will be revealed," when God will "render to each according to his works" (2:5–6). Those who persevere in "good work" in order to gain "glory and honor and immortality" will receive the "life of the age," which consists in "glory and honor and peace" (2:7, 10).[4] Those, however, who are disobedient towards the truth out of selfish ambition, who instead obey unrighteousness, who work evil, will receive wrath and fury, tribulation and distress—the Jew first, and then the Greek (2:8–9). What does Paul have in mind here? Is this a storm to end all storms—in J. D. G. Dunn's words, a "final judgment on human rebellion"?[5] Or will it eventually pass by, leaving the landscape of history devastated, transformed, but otherwise intact? Dunn observes that in Jewish thought "divine wrath is not a particularly eschatological concept," by which he means that it is usually descriptive of a historical event "with special reference to the covenant relation," rather than of a final or cosmic event. He argues, however, that there are exceptions to this general rule (e.g., Isa 13:9, 13; Zeph 1:15, 18; 2:2–3; 3:8; Dan 8:19; *Jub.* 24.30), which look beyond the contingencies of history and envisage a "final judgment that is simply the end of a pro-

---

4. By translating *zōē aiōnios* as "life of the age" rather than the customary "eternal life" we highlight the fact that this is a life associated with the age to come and not simply life in heaven after death.

5. Dunn, *Romans 1–8*, 84. Cf. Fitzmyer, *Romans*, 108: "From such a Jewish background Paul derives the notion of God's wrath, which he now associates with God's cosmic judgment."

cess already in train" (e.g., *1 En.* 84.4; 91.7–9). Against this background it appears that "Paul is shifting from a narrower covenant perspective to a more cosmic or universal perspective, from God understood primarily as the God of Israel to God as Creator of all."[6] This conclusion needs to be challenged. It is not clear either that the Jewish texts envisage a final judgment in this sense or that the covenantal and cosmic aspects of Paul's theology are to be differentiated—and seemingly dissociated—in this way. Indeed, the argument developed here will be that in Paul's mind the universal political-religious sovereignty of God is to be established in the medium term through a historically complex renewal of the covenant, and that the genuinely transcendent cosmic hope occupies only a peripheral and indeterminate place in his account of future outcomes.

The Day of Wrath in the Old Testament and Jewish Thought

Isaiah describes an "incurable day of the Lord," a "day of wrath and anger," that is coming "to make the whole *oikoumenē* desolate and to destroy the sinners from it" (Isa 13:9 LXX; cf. 13:13). The passage is cited by Dunn as an exception to the sub-eschatological or historical conception of wrath, but it forms part of an oracle concerning the *oikoumenē* of Babylon: it describes the coming overthrow of Israel's arch enemy by the Medes. The other passages listed are similarly unexceptional. In language that closely foreshadows Paul's own phraseology, Zephaniah predicts an attack on Jerusalem that will be a "day of wrath . . . of distress and anguish" (Zeph 1:15; cf. 1:18). This is not a "last day" or "final judgment" in any absolute or suprahistorical sense. English versions of Zephaniah 1:18 typically universalize the "day of the wrath of the Lord" by translating *kol-ha'arets* as "all the earth." Both the Hebrew *'arets* and the Greek *gē* can mean either "earth" or "land," but here the context clearly disambiguates in favor of "land." This is the imminent "great day of the Lord," when he will stretch out his hand "against Judah and against all the inhabitants of Jerusalem" (1:4, 14), when those who are humble and seek righteousness may perhaps be preserved (2:2–3; cf. Lam 1:12; 2:21–22, 24). It is the *land*, therefore, that in the first place will be "consumed by the fire of his

---

6. Dunn, *Romans 1–8*, 54. Moo states: "Although Jewish apocalyptic conceived of the transition from old age to new as taking place in the field of actual history, Paul's conception is necessarily more nuanced" (Moo, *Romans*, 26).

jealousy" and the inhabitants of the *land* who will suffer sudden destruction. Subsequently, there will be a judgment on the nations, when God will pour out "my indignation, all my burning anger" on the enemies of Judah (3:8), but nothing suggests that we have arrived here at the perilous rim of world history and must inevitably sail over the edge.[7] Daniel is told what will happen "at the end of the wrath against the sons of your people" (Dan 8:19 LXX), but the climax in view is the deliverance of the righteous in Israel from the hands of the overweening pagan aggressor when the period of protracted exile finally comes to a close and the oppressed, faithful *saints* of the Most High are vindicated—in the person of the "son of man" figure—before the throne of God.[8]

Far from hinting at a final judgment, *Jubilees* 24.30 points emphatically towards a conception of "wrath" as theological redescription of historical events. Isaac has cursed the Philistines: they are to be an object of "wrath and anger at the hands of the sinners, the nations, and in the hands of the Kittim"; those who escape the sword of the Kittim will be eradicated by the Jews (24.28–29). None of the Philistines will survive the "day of the wrath of judgment" (24.30). Two passages from *1 Enoch* are cited as evidence of a final judgment that comes as the climax to a period of wrath. The wrath of God "shall rest upon the flesh of the people until . . . the great day of judgment" (84.4). When oppression and injustice reach their peak, the "holy Lord shall emerge with wrath and plague in order that he may execute judgment upon the earth"; sinners will be destroyed, cut off by the sword, delivered into the hands of the righteous (91.7–12). Significantly, this "righteous judgment" will then be revealed to the whole world—exactly as Paul speaks of a revelation of the righteousness of God—and "all people shall direct their sight to the path of uprightness" (91.14). This strongly suggests that this day of wrath is directed not against the whole world but specifically against the wicked in Israel who oppress the righteous. *1 Enoch* 91.9 speaks of the abandon-

---

7. It may be a day when God shatters the kings who oppose his anointed ruler (Ps 110:5); also Mic 5:15. Ezekiel paints a vivid picture of a "day of the wrath of the Lord" (Ezek 7:19), when those caught outside the city will die from the sword and those inside the city will die of famine and disease: their wealth—the "stumbling block of their iniquity"—will not save them because there will be no food to buy. The temple will be profaned by foreigners. The worst of nations will take possession of their houses. "According to their way I will do to them, and according to their judgments I will judge them, and they shall know that I am the Lord" (Ezek 7:27).

8. See Perriman, *Son of Man*, 9–13.

ment of "All that is (common) with the heathen": that is, everything that unrighteous Jews have in common with pagans, such as the worship of idols, will be destroyed.[9]

It is not clear, therefore, that the language of a "day of wrath" would have evoked either in Paul's mind or in the minds of his Jewish audience the thought of a "last judgment" or "final Assize."[10] In fact, the text that appears most consistently to have informed his argument about the wrath of God in Romans is Deuteronomy 28–32, which keeps us firmly in the realm of a historically circumscribed, covenantal understanding of the judgment that Paul foresees. The phrase "tribulation and distress" (*thlipsis kai stenochōria*) in Romans 2:9 occurs three times in inverted form in Deuteronomy 28, where it evokes not a mythical or final disorder but the sufferings inflicted on the people of God by an enemy—when the cities of Israel are besieged by the nation that the Lord will bring against them in judgment (Deut 28:53, 55, 57 LXX; cf. Isa 8:22; 30:6). The causal link between Law and wrath in Romans 4:15 has its origins in texts such as Deuteronomy 29:25–28 LXX: if Israel abandons the covenant and serves other gods, the Lord will be angry (*ōrgisthē*) with that land and will bring upon it all the curses written in the book of the Law; "the Lord removed them from their land in wrath and anger (*thymō kai orgē*) and very great provocation and cast them into another land, as it is now" (Deut 29:28). The pairing of *orgē* and *thymos* is found in Romans 2:8. Israel is solemnly warned that if the people are led astray to worship other gods and serve them, they "will perish with destruction" (*apōleia apoleisthe*); when they provoke God to jealousy with their idols, a "day of destruction will be near to them" (Deut 30:18; 32:21, 35, my translation). Paul speaks of the Jews as having become "vessels of wrath prepared for destruction (*apōleian*)" (Rom 9:22). Finally, as part of his teaching on how to respond as a community to hostility and persecution, Paul urges the saints in Rome not to seek to avenge themselves against their persecutors but to "leave it to the wrath, for it is written, 'Vengeance is mine, I will repay,' says the

---

9. The elect will inherit the earth; they will "not be judged all the days of their lives; nor die through plague or wrath," but will live to old age (1 *En.* 5.9). When the Son of Man is revealed, the "holy ones" will be established before him, but rulers—kings, governors, high officials and landlords—will be punished because they have oppressed the elect; the "wrath of the Lord of Spirits shall rest upon them"; and the righteous will rejoice because their oppressors have been destroyed (62.1–16).

10. Against Wright, *Justification*, 158.

Lord'" (12:14–19). The quotation is from a passage in Deuteronomy 32 that speaks of a day of calamity and doom, when the Lord will "judge his people," when he will "avenge the blood of his sons and take revenge and repay the enemies with a sentence," when he will "repay those who hate, and . . . cleanse the land of his people" (Deut 32:35–36, 43 LXX; cf. Jer 28:6).

The same basic picture emerges when we consider passages that link, as Paul does (Rom 2:5), the day of wrath with the "righteous judgment" (*dikaiokrisia*) of God. *Testament of Levi* 3.1–3 speaks of a "day determined by God's righteous judgment (*dikaiokrisiai*)," when the unrighteous deeds of people will be punished, when vengeance will be worked "on the spirits of error and of Beliar." The accompanying imagery has a cosmic aspect to it, but the outcome is a new age, when Beliar will have been bound (*T. Levi* 18.12; cf. Rev 20:2), when Israel will be blessed as a light to the nations, and the marginalized God of Israel will "visit all the nations forever" (*T. Levi* 4.4; 14.3–4). In a later passage the word is used with reference to the desolation of the sanctuary and the captivity of Israel (15.2).

In *Sibylline Oracles* the defeat of Rome by Antony, Lepidus, and Octavian is described as a day of "implacable wrath," of the "judgment (*krisis*) of the great immortal God," when "All men will perish in their own dwellings when the fiery cataract flows from heaven" (3.51–56). A "heavenly eternal destruction" will come upon Babylon and on the "children of wrath" (3.307–9), and on the Greeks, who "give vain gifts to the dead and sacrifice to idols," who "abandon the face of the great God and do these things" (3.547–49, 556). Devious mortals must "guard against the wrath of the great God, whenever the culmination of pestilence comes upon all mortals and they are subdued and meet with terrible justice" (3.624, 632–34). When the kings of the peoples make a final assault against Jerusalem, "judgment will come upon them from the great God, and all will perish at the hand of the Immortal"; the "sons of the great God," however, will live peacefully around the temple, they will be free from war; and the islands and cities will acknowledge how much the Immortal loves his people, they will praise God, and say, "Let us send to the Temple, since he alone is sovereign and let us all ponder the Law of the Most High God, who is most righteous of all throughout the earth" (3.718–20). These texts present an apocalyptically heightened form of the hope frequently expressed in the Psalms and the Prophets that the righteousness of God will be demonstrated to the world through overwhelming historical events (e.g., Ps 97:2, 9; Isa 52:10 LXX).

God Judges the Secrets of Men: 2:16

Finally, this is a day when "according to my gospel, God judges the secrets of men by Christ Jesus" (Rom 2:16). We naturally hear this as the language of a universal and personal final judgment, but it takes on a quite different complexion when the background lighting of a highly pertinent intertextual context is switched on. To take an Old Testament example first, Jeremiah speaks of the sin of Judah being "engraved on the tablet of their heart" on account of their idolatry; they will be made to "serve your enemies in a land that you do not know." When this happens, those who rely on men will be cursed; the exile will be for them a wilderness experience. But those who trust in the Lord will be blessed: they will be like trees planted by water; they will continue to be fruitful even in exile. Then Jeremiah writes: "The heart is deceitful above all things, and desperately sick; who can understand it? 'I the Lord search the heart and test the mind, to give every man according to his ways, according to the fruit of his deeds'" (Jer 17:9–10). This searching of the heart will have consequences. The Jew who *at this time*—under these conditions of judgment—has acquired riches by unjust means will lose them "in the midst of his days," and will end up a fool. Those who forsake the Lord *at this time*—like the scribes and Pharisees who brought the woman caught in adultery to Jesus to be condemned—"shall be written in the earth" (17:11–13; John 8:8).

Hellenistic Judaism, however, provides the more telling parallels. Wisdom of Solomon warns blasphemers that they will not escape detection "because God is a witness of their inner feelings and a true overseer of their hearts"; they will receive punishment "in accordance with the way they reasoned" (Wis 1:6; 3:10–12). The writer of the *Psalms of Solomon* reflects on the exile as evidence of the righteousness of God, that he is a "righteous judge over all the peoples of the earth": neither the righteous nor the unrighteous are hidden from God's knowledge. He then argues that it is within Israel's power to choose to do right or to do wrong. The one who does right "stores up (*thēsaurizei*) life for himself with the Lord"; the one who does wrong "forfeits the source of his life in destruction" (*en apōleiai*)" (*Pss. Sol.* 9.1–5, my translation). In a later psalm it is said that the inheritance of the unrighteous will be "Hades, and darkness and destruction (*apōleia*)," because God "knows the secrets of the heart before they happen" (*Pss. Sol.* 14.6–10).[11] Finally, perhaps against the background of Pompey's incursion into Jerusalem (63 BC),[12] the psalmist calls on God to raise up a king, a son of David, who will destroy the unrighteous rulers of Israel and "purge Jerusalem from gentiles." There are distinct echoes of Psalm 2 here: the king will "smash the arrogance of sinners like a potter's jar . . . shatter all their substance with an iron rod." Then at his rebuke "the nations will flee from his presence; and he will condemn sinners by the thoughts of their hearts" (*Pss. Sol.* 17.21–25).

My contention here is not that Paul is uncritically restating the outlook of Hellenistic Judaism. The belief that Jesus had been raised from the dead must clearly have provoked a radical re-evaluation of the various narratives by which Judaism sought to explain how the God of Israel was dealing with the plight of his people with respect to the religious and political hegemony of Greco-Roman paganism. But these texts are still indicative of the intellectual environment within which Paul engaged constructively and imaginatively with the Jews of the *oikoumenē* and *as a Jew himself* with Gentiles; and the question still has to be asked whether his gospel really forces a fundamental translation of the biblical language of wrath, of tribulation and distress, of a righteous judgment of the secrets of men's hearts, into final or cosmic terms. Is the resurrection of Jesus a matter of such theological and metaphysical novelty that it rewrites the terms of the whole debate? Or do we make better sense of the argument in Romans if we resist the tendency to tear the event from the fabric of a realistic and urgent narrative about the historical fate of the people of God, loosely woven from biblical prophecy and Jewish apocalypticism?

For now it seems to me that there is nothing in Paul's appropriation of this language to indicate that he thought of the day of God's wrath as a final judgment at the end of history—as *fin du monde* rather than *fin de siècle*. This does not preclude, dogmatically speaking, a final judgment of all the dead—this is what we find described, I think, in a rather different apocalyptic idiom, in Revelation 20:11–15. The point is simply that this is not what Paul is talking about when he puts forward the case to both Jews

11. Or better: the Lord "knows the secret rooms (*tamieia*) of the heart before it happens."

12. Charlesworth, *Pseudepigrapha*, 640–41.

and Greeks that God has fixed a day when he will judge the *oikoumenē* in righteousness.

Jesus and the Wrath of God

We also need to insert Jesus's understanding of the judgment of God somewhere in the interpretive tradition that runs from the Old Testament through the theologies of Second Temple Judaism to Paul. In Luke's Gospel John the Baptist berates the crowds that come to be baptized: "Who warned you to flee from the wrath to come?" (Luke 3:7; cf. Matt 3:7). It is not enough to claim Abraham as your father: "Even now the axe is laid to the root of the trees." Later Jesus speaks of the coming war as a time of "great distress upon the land (*epi tēs gēs*) and wrath against this people" (my translation), when Jerusalem will be surrounded by armies, Judeans will fall by the sword and be taken into captivity, and the city will be trampled under foot by foreigners (Luke 21:23–24). This is the calamity that John had in mind—when "every tree that does not bear good fruit is cut down and thrown into the fire" (Luke 3:9). Even in John's Gospel we can discern through the layers of metaphysical varnish an underlying eschatological realism. The statement "whoever does not obey the Son shall not see life, but the wrath of God remains on him" belongs to a reflection on the significance of John the Baptist (John 3:36). It fits the wider, not entirely suppressed, narrative of a judgment that will be executed by the Son of Man, when those in the tombs—there is no reason to look beyond Israel here—will be raised, those who have done good, to life, those who have done evil, to judgment (John 5:25–29; cf. 9:35–41; 12:31–34). The Pharisees and chief priests warn the Sanhedrin that if the Jesus movement gets out of control, "the Romans will come and take away both our place (*arousin hēmōn . . . ton topon*) and our nation"—in Caiaphas's words, the nation will "perish" (John 11:48, 50). There is at least a hint here of Daniel's account of the military leader who will "take away their place (*exērthē ho topos autōn*) and sacrifice," leaving the sanctuary desolated, which is part of the outworking of the "wrath against the sons of your people" (Dan 8:11, 19 LXX, my translation).[13]

---

13. This is probably not incompatible with the view that the Sanhedrin is primarily afraid that the Romans will take the temple and the nation out of their control (Beasley-Murray, *John*, 196).

If the catastrophe of AD 66–70 dominated Jesus's eschatological horizon as the predicted vindication of his message and of the course of action that he pursued, are we to suppose that this expectation has left no impression at all on Paul's eschatology? When he writes—clearly in a state of intense anxiety regarding the likely fate of his brothers according to the flesh (9:1–3)—to the churches in Rome in the mid-50s about a day of wrath that would bring affliction and anguish upon the Jew first, upon a people portrayed as "vessels of wrath prepared for destruction" (Rom 9:22), should we not assume that he had a national calamity of just this nature and these dimensions in mind? Is it likely that he would have echoed YHWH's complaint that he has stretched out his hands "all day to a disobedient and contrary people" (Rom 10:21; cf. Isa 62:2 LXX) without recalling the awful consequence: "I will destine you to the sword, and all of you shall bow down to the slaughter, because, when I called, you did not answer; when I spoke, you did not listen, but you did what was evil in my eyes and chose what I did not delight in" (Isa 65:12)? Why should the wrath to come have been different in kind to the wrath of God that, as Paul explained to the Thessalonians, had already in some form or other come upon the Jews utterly or at last (1 Thess 2:16)? This curious formulation is found almost verbatim in *T. Levi* 6.11 (*ephthase de hē orgē kuriou ep' autous eis telos*), where it serves to interpret the slaughter of the Shechemites by Levi and his brothers as an act of divine judgment against them for their mistreatment of strangers. If Paul has in mind the expulsion of the Jews from Rome by Claudius in AD 49 (Acts 18:2; Suetonius *Claud.* 25.4) or the massacre by Rome of thousands of Jews in the temple during the Passover festival in the same year (Josephus *J.W.* 2.224–27), the conclusion must surely be reached, given the purview of his argument with the Jews of the diaspora, that the wrath to come will take the form of the much greater devastation of Israel by Rome in the war of AD 66–70.

5

Jews and Greeks and the Things They Have Done

The premise of Paul's argument in Romans is that the wrath of God is coming upon a world that has been given over to immorality and unrighteousness because somewhere back in the mists of time it chose to worship man-made idols rather than the Creator. The outcome remains historically undefined—there is nothing comparable to Jesus's quite detailed and plausible prediction of a war against Rome culminating in the besieging of Jerusalem. But the consistent literary dependence on Old Testament narratives of judgment and vindication creates the strong impression that Paul has in mind something comparable to earlier, archetypal instances of upheaval, destruction, and transition.

The impact of this day of wrath will be felt by the Jew first, then by the Greek. The distinction reflects the Old Testament pattern, seen not least in Habakkuk, of judgment on Israel and Jerusalem followed by judgment on the merciless foreign aggressor; and it paves the way for the particular—and for the defense of Paul's gospel, critical—focus on Jewish presumption that begins at 2:17. But the argument has been constructed to this point in such a way that his Jewish auditors are likely to have caught a disturbing glimpse of their own image in the mirror that has been held up to paganism. Israel is barely less culpable than the nations when it comes to idolatry, unrighteousness, moral complacency, and, if truth be told, contempt for the God whose forbearance is meant to lead to repentance. To that extent the day of wrath, whatever historical shape it may take, will be impartial. Both Jews and Greeks must expect their world to be turned upside down, and how that affects them will be determined by what they have done: "There will be tribulation and distress for every human being who does evil, the Jew first and also the Greek, but glory and honor and peace for everyone who does good, the Jew first and also the Greek" (Rom 2:9–10).

If we suppose that at the heart of Paul's theology is a doctrine of universal personal salvation from the consequences of a final judgment on the basis of faith rather than of works, this account of things is patently an embarrassment, in two respects. First, the language of a "day of wrath" and the repeated reference to the "Greek," rather than to some broader category of general humanity, would appear to circumscribe the judgment both geographically and temporally. Secondly, this is clearly a judgment according to what people have done; and Paul appears to believe that people will be justified on this day of wrath by virtue of the fact that they have done the things of the Law (2:13–14). Quite how this embarrassment is to be resolved will not become clear until later in the letter. For now it is important to let this foundational passage stand as it is without subjecting it to hasty theological qualification.

Why Just the Greeks?

There is a prominent apocalyptic background to the focus on the opposition of Jew and Greek, going back to conflicts foreseen by Daniel and Zechariah (cf. Dan 11:29–31; Zech 9:13). Antiochus is, in Jewish memory, the monstrous epitome of Greek antipathy towards Israel and the covenant (cf. 1 Macc 8:17–18; 4 Macc 18:20). In a passage that echoes Paul's argument in Romans 2:12–16, *Sibylline Oracles* foresees a day when "No longer will the unclean foot of Greeks revel around your land but they will have a mind in their breasts that conforms to your laws" (*Sib. Or.* 5.264; cf. 3.632–41). This is a post-Neronic oracle, so "Greeks" clearly denotes Rome as the great eschatological antagonist.

This antagonism, centered on the looming revolt against Roman occupation, lies behind Paul's argument: wrath against the Jews will be followed, sooner or later, by wrath against the Greeks. Notice has been served on a dominant and overweening culture that long ago "exchanged the glory of the immortal God for images resembling mortal man and birds and animals and creeping things" (Rom 1:23), which has been handed over to depravity and unrighteousness as a sign of divine displeasure, and whose long history of aggression towards YHWH and his people has yet to reach its climax. As Paul explained to the men of Athens on the Areopagus, the resurrection of Jesus is a clear sign that the current political-religious arrangement cannot go on for ever: the Creator God has "fixed a day on which he will judge the world (*oikoumenēn*) in righteousness" (Acts 17:31). This is the language of the Psalms: "the Lord remains for ever; he prepared his throne in judgment . . . it is he who will judge the world in righteousness (*krinei tēn oikoumenēn en dikaiosynē*); he will judge peoples with uprightness" (Ps 9:8–9 LXX); ". . . he is coming to judge the earth. He will judge the world with righteousness (*krinei tēn oikoumenēn en dikaiosynē*) and peoples in his truth" (Ps 95:13; cf. 97:9 LXX). What these texts assert, however, is not a *final* judgment of all humanity but the continuing sovereignty of YHWH, who is king above all gods and who, therefore, will act whenever necessary *in history* to defend the needy or deliver his people from their enemies. He will judge the Greco-Roman *oikoumenē* in the same way that he judged and punished the Egyptians for having oppressed Israel (cf. Gen 15:14; Acts 7:7) or the Assyrians and Chaldeans—"according to their deeds and the work of their hands"—for having arrogantly exceeded their remit as agents of God's wrath against Israel (Isa 10:12, 15; Jer 25:12–14, 17–26; Hab 2:15–16).

A Word, Somewhat Belatedly, about Oikoumenē

The word *oikoumenē* signifies the inhabited world. It can be used in a general sense in Jewish texts without consciousness of administrative boundaries, differing little in that respect from *kosmos* (e.g., Pss 17:6; 18:5; 96:4; 97:7); but it may also have a more precise frame of reference. In Josephus it effectively denotes the geographical extent of the Roman Empire.[1] He records, for example, an incident in which the emperor Tiberius is informed of a treasonable statement that Agrippa had made to Caius: "I hope that the day will at length arrive when this old man will leave the scene and appoint you ruler of the world (*oikoumenēs*)!" (Josephus *Ant.* 18.187, LCL). In the Old Testament *oikoumenē* sometimes clearly has a restricted scope. In an oracle against Babylon Isaiah writes that God

---

1. Otherwise, words denoting "rule" or "authority" are used, such as *hēgemonia* or *archē*.

has commanded a heavily armed nation to come from a distant land and destroy the whole *oikoumenē* and make the whole *oikoumenē* desolate (Isa 13:4–5, 9, 17–19). The Medes do not destroy the whole world; they destroy the empire of the Chaldeans. When Nebuchadnezzar is described in Daniel as "king of kings and ruling the whole *oikoumenē*" (Dan 3:2), the word in effect defines the extent of the emperor's sovereignty.

The geopolitical dimensions of the term are no less apparent in the New Testament. Luke tells us at the beginning of the story of Jesus that "a decree went out from Caesar Augustus that all the *oikoumenēn* should be registered" (Luke 2:1); the *oikoumenē* is the world that Caesar rules. We should probably hear the same connotation in Satan's offer to give the nations of the *oikoumenē* to Jesus, and in Jesus's apocalyptic account of the distress that will come upon the *oikoumenē* when the Son of Man is vindicated (Luke 21:25–26). Agabus warns of a famine that will afflict the whole *oikoumenē* or "empire"—Luke comments that this took place in the days of the emperor Claudius (Acts 11:28). The men who supposedly have "turned the *oikoumenēn* upside down" have acted "against the decrees of Caesar, saying that there is another king, Jesus" (Acts 17:6–7). The association between the *oikoumenē* and the sphere of classical paganism is apparent from the words of Demetrius the silversmith regarding the great goddess Artemis—"she whom all Asia and the *oikoumenē* worship" (Acts 19:27).

For Luke the *oikoumenē* is the Greco-Roman world, which suggests that when he has Paul on the Areopagus, overlooking the home of classical paganism, declare with considerable temerity that the end is in sight for a religious system that mistakes the works of human hands for divinity, that the *oikoumenē* is soon to be judged—overthrown, shown to be worthless, rendered obsolete—by a man whom the one true God has appointed, we should take seriously the political, social, and religious parameters of the expectation. This most powerful and destructive pagan culture has so far been allowed to make war with impunity against the covenant people, but the time is approaching when the great empire will be judged and "the authority and the kingdom and the magnitude of all the kingdoms, which are under heaven" will be given to the victims of pagan aggression—to the saints of the Most High (Dan 7:27 LXX). In Daniel's vision the first three beasts are permitted to survive the judgment, but the fourth beast, which is so naturally interpreted in Jewish apocalyptic tradition as a Greek imperialism that becomes a Roman imperialism, is killed and its corpse destroyed in the fire that issued from the throne of God (Dan 7:11–12). In its place the saints of the Most High come to reign—and I wonder whether it is really too fanciful to suggest that this apocalyptically conceived hope, reconfigured by Jesus's identification of himself and his followers with the figure like a son of man who comes on the clouds of heaven, found fulfillment in the victory of Christ over the gods, represented historically—and therefore, of course, *ambiguously*—by Constantine's adoption of Christianity as the religion of the empire.

The lines of New Testament expectation converge, with only a few outlying exceptions that foresee a renewal of all creation, on a two-stage historical outcome—with respect to the Jew, first, and then the Greek. The climax comes as a final transfer of sovereignty from the domineering and demonic hierarchy of imperial paganism to Jesus, who did not count equality with God a thing to be grasped, who made himself of no account, took the form of a servant, the form of a son of man, who became obedient to the point of death, was repudiated by apostate Judaism, and was executed by Rome in advance of the thousands who would be crucified during the war.

A Judgment according to Works: 2:5–11

On this day of judgment God will render both to the Jew and to the Greek "according to their works" (Rom 2:6). The first point to be made is that the argument here is not that the basis for judgment will be works *rather than faith*, but that judgment will take a form *corresponding to*—in accordance with—what people have done, which makes sense only if we suppose that Paul has concrete social outcomes in view. The thought is readily illustrated from Jewish writings. For example, in Psalm 27:4–5 LXX (= Ps 28:4–5) it is said that God will give to the wicked "according to their works." Because they disregarded the works of the Lord, he will "bring them down and build them up no more"—that is, if they reduce the work of God's hand to nothing, he will reduce them to nothing. The punishment fits the crime. Those in Israel who oppress the righteous, Isaiah declares, will have to "eat the fruit of their works." "Woe to the lawless one! Evil things will happen to him according to the works (*kata ta erga*) of his hands" (Isa 3:9–11). Even more clearly, Jeremiah calls for

Babylon to be repaid (*antapodote*) "according to her works" (*kata ta erga autēs*): "just as she has done, do to her—because she withstood the Lord, holy God of Israel. Therefore her young men shall fall in her squares, and all her fighting men shall be thrown down, said the Lord" (Jer 27:29–30; cf. Lam 3:64–66). The nation that destroys Israel by war will itself be destroyed by war.[2]

Ben Sirach states: "According to his great mercy, so also is his reproof; he will judge a man according to his deeds (*kata ta erga autou*)." The sinner, therefore, will not escape with his booty; and the "endurance of the pious will never fail" (Sir 16:12–13). The writer of the *Psalms of Solomon* justifies God because he is righteous in his judgments, because he has "rewarded the sinners according to their actions"—not in a final judgment but by exposing the sins of unrighteous Israel and expunging their "memory from the earth" by means of foreign invasion (*Pss. Sol.* 2.15–21). Just as the nations overthrew the kingdom of David, so God "overthrew them, and uprooted their descendants from the earth"; in this way God repaid them according to their sins, so that it "happened to them according to their actions (*kata ta erga autōn*)." This is one of the judgments of the Lord, "which he makes in the world" (*Pss. Sol.* 17.6–10). Wisdom of Solomon, finally, gives warning to the impious that they will "receive punishment in accordance with the way they reasoned": those who disdain wisdom will find that their hope is in vain, their labors unprofitable, their actions useless, their wives foolish, and their children evil (Wis 3:10–12).

Paul's argument here is little different. The Jew who regards his Greek neighbor with contempt is actually in the same boat, heading into the same storm: because of his hard and impenitent heart, he too is "storing up (*thēsaurizeis*) wrath" for himself on the day of wrath (Rom 2:5). The metaphor reinforces the moral connection between what a person does and the manner of repayment. "The one who does what is right saves up (*thēsaurizei*) life for himself with the Lord, and the one who does what is wrong causes his own life to be destroyed; for the Lord's righteous

2. Paul makes a point of quoting the last line of Psalm 62: on the envisaged day of wrath God will "render to each one according to his works." More clearly in the Greek version than in the Hebrew, the Psalm is an exhortation to the "congregation of people" to trust in God and a condemnation of those who acquire wealth by robbery. In the end, God "will repay to each according to his works" (Ps 61:9–12 LXX). See also Prov 24:12; Job 34:11; Jer 17:10; Hos 12:2; *1 En.* 100.7; *Jos. Asen.* 28.3; Ps-Philo *Lib. Ant.* 3.10.

judgments are according to the individual and the household" (*Pss. Sol.* 9.5). Those who "by patience in well-doing seek for glory and honor and immortality," Paul argues, will be repaid *in accordance with* their works with the life of the age to come, with "glory and honor and peace." Those who suppress the truth, who let themselves be corrupted by the unrighteous, will be repaid, in accordance with their works, with "tribulation and distress."

The word that stands out here is "immortality" or imperishability (*aphtharsian*). This is certainly not merely a social good: it refers to a genuine resurrection life (cf. 1 Cor 15:42; 15:50, 53–54; Eph 6:24; 2 Tim 1:10; 4 Macc 17:12). But the social dimension is not thereby simply transcended, as though the ultimate prospect in view were the immortality of the individual. It derives from a corporate aspiration: it refers to the hope that Israel has of not being finally destroyed because its God is incorruptible. Imperishability is what survives the savage torture inflicted by Antiochus Epiphanes (4 Macc 9:22; 17:12). In the context of an argument about the wrath of God that is so thoroughly shaped by a Jewish narrative of judgment and vindication, the reward of "life of the age" (*zōēn aiōnion*) that is given to those who "by patience in well-doing seek for glory and honor and immortality" presupposes an eschatological transition that will eventually see a faithful community vindicated and the idolatrous and unrighteous *oikoumenē* overthrown.

Hearers and Doers of the Law: 2:12–16

Because this is about the Jew first and then the Greek, the Law inevitably becomes an issue. Those who sinned lawlessly (*anomōs*) will perish lawlessly; those who sinned under the Law will be judged according to the terms of the Law. In the imagined courtroom of this day of wrath the claim merely to have *heard* the Law will not count as any defense; only those who have *done* what the Law requires will be justified before God. Paul might have appealed to Scripture at this point to back up his case (Ezek 33:31–32, for example), but he does not. Instead, he makes a straightforward observation as a matter of practical morality: if non-Jews do "by nature" the good works that the Law requires from Jews, then clearly in some sense it can be said that they are the Law to themselves; they show that the *work* of the Law is written on their hearts (Rom 2:14–15).

These are not Gentile Christians.[3] First, it is the *work* of the Law that is written on their hearts, not the Law itself. Jeremiah writes of a time when YHWH will make a new covenant with the house of Israel: "I will put my law within them, and I will write it on their hearts" (Jer 31:33). Paul uses the metaphor in a rather different sense in 2 Corinthians: through the work of the apostles, who are ministers of a new covenant, the Corinthian believers have become a "letter from Christ . . . written not with ink but with the Spirit of the living God, not on tablets of stone but on tablets of human hearts" (2 Cor 3:3). Secondly, the work of the Law by which Gentiles might be justified is inspired not by the Spirit but "by nature" (*physei*).[4] Thirdly, the appeal to conscience and to the testimony presented by their conflicting thoughts makes no sense if these are Christians who know that they are justified in Christ and no longer subject to condemnation. Presumably, then, Paul has in mind Gentiles such as the centurion Cornelius before his conversion, who is described by the Jews as a "righteous man who fears God"—there is no reason to think that Paul would have disputed their opinion of him (Acts 10:22).

The argument of 2:1–16 has to be taken at face value. There will be a day of wrath in the course of history when God will judge the *oikoumenē* by the risen Jesus, to whom he will give as an inheritance the nations, wrested from the power of the gods—from the emperor who imagines equality with God a thing to be grasped for himself, down to the most parochial deities of woodland and village. Biblically speaking, judgment denotes concrete outcomes, determined by what people have done. Those who have done good works in the hope of gaining glory, honor, and immortality will receive the glory, honor, and peace that will characterize the life of the age to come. Those who have disobeyed the truth and done what is evil will experience affliction and distress: they will perish in the sense that communities, nations, and civilizations in the past have perished. The Jew must understand that the rift will open not along the

---

3. Against Wright, *Romans*, 441–42; Wright, *Justification*, 166–67.

4. The point is certainly debatable. It is possible that "by nature" is meant to modify the having of the Law rather than the doing of the work of the Law. But sentence structure weighs against this (cf. Fitzmyer, *Romans*, 310), and it is questionable whether it makes sense to say that Gentiles do not possess—or implicitly that Jews do possess—the Law "by nature." In the two obvious parallel instances in Paul *ek physeōs* and *physei* are enclosed within the clause which they modify (Rom 2:27; Gal 2:15); and being circumcised and being Jews are *natural* conditions in a way that having the Law is not.

boundary between those who have the Law and those who do not; rather it will divide those who do the *work* of the Law from those who do not.

So far this is an argument purely about the wrath of God and its implications for the Jew and the Greek. Paul will say nothing about an alternative outcome determined by faith(fulness) until Romans 3:21–22. The question arises at that point because he has declared that no Jew will be justified by works of the Law (3:20), with the result that the nation of Abraham's descendants is faced with destruction. In outline, and in anticipation of the more substantial discussion to come, we may set out the underlying reasoning as follows. The God of Israel has fixed a day on which he will vindicate himself as God of the whole world before the peoples of the *oikoumenē* by judging the whole system of Greco-Roman paganism. To do that with integrity, however, he must first judge his own people, who should have constituted a benchmark for righteousness in the midst of the nations. So both the Jew and the Greek will be judged according to what they have done.

But now a different problem arises. Paul sees that by staking a claim to the whole earth in this way, God is in danger of reneging on the promise made to Abraham that his descendants would be blessed and would be a blessing to the nations. This is the point in the deep logic of Paul's reconstruction of his gospel in Romans at which an alternative path becomes necessary. A community has been called into existence apart from the Law and in advance of the coming day of wrath *as a concrete demonstration of the intentions of God*. It exists in the time leading up to the judgment of the *oikoumenē* only on the basis of faith(fulness), for two reasons. On the one hand, it is made up of Jews, first, but also Greeks, who have had to abandon their old allegiances and trust or believe in the narrow path determined by Jesus's story. On the other, this is a community that, as a consequence of its consistent witness to the God who has given Jesus the nations as an inheritance, will have to endure with faith(fulness) the same hatred and violence that Jesus endured. It is because God will judge both Jews and Greeks according to their works, on the basis of what they have done, that he has brought into existence a community that must live by faith(fulness) if it is going to serve its purpose in this time of momentous historical transition.

Sibylline Oracles, *Wrath against Israel and Rome,* and the Prize of Immortality

This is merely a sketch at this point of how this unfamiliar eschatological narrative may help us to rethink the argument of Romans. We can take this process of reconceptualization a step further by considering a passage in the *Sibylline Oracles* (dated by Charlesworth between AD 70 and AD 150). An insertion by a Christian redactor describes how the Jews will "reap the bad harvest" when they launch a haughty and reckless rebellion against Rome. As a consequence the temple of Solomon will be destroyed, and the "Hebrews will be driven from their land; wandering, being slaughtered, they will mix much darnel in their wheat." This will be the wrath of God—punishment for an evil deed (*Sib. Or.* 1.387–400; cf. 1.362). The Jewish text then describes a tenth and last generation of men, when God will "break the glory of idols and shake the people of seven-hilled Rome" and "impose famines and pestilence and thunderbolts on men who adjudicate without justice." But God will save "pious men"; there will be "deep peace and understanding" and "shamelessness will perish" (2.15–33). A crown from heaven in the form of a bright star will then be revealed, to be won in a contest, at which point we revert to the Christian redaction. People from all nations will strive to win the prize of immortality. Christ will give, on the one hand, an "immortal treasure" to the martyrs who "pursue the contest even to death" and, on the other, an "imperishable (*aphtharton*) prize" to "virgins who run well and to all men who perform justice and to diverse nations who live piously and acknowledge one God" (2.39–52; cf. 2.149–53).

The contest to attain the "fame of immortality" (*kleos athanasiēs*, my translation) will be for the whole world (*oikoumenikos*), for every people; similarly Paul speaks of those from among both Jews and Greeks who "seek for glory and honor and immortality" (*Sib. Or.* 2.40–43; Rom 2:7). Christ is the judge in both texts (*Sib. Or.* 2.45–46; Rom 2:16). Just as Paul expects "life of the age" to be given to those who persevere in good works, who do the work of the Law, the holy Christ of the *Sibylline Oracles* will "give an imperishable (*aphtharton*) prize" and an "eternal hope" to "virgins (*parthenikois*) who run well and to all men who perform justice and to diverse nations who live piously and acknowledge one God, who love marriage and refrain from adultery" (*Sib. Or.* 2.48–52). Importantly, the

Oracles also give priority to a specific group—the martyrs who "pursue the contest even to death" (2.46–47). This is not, on the face of it, equivalent to a group that is justified by faith(fulness), but we will see that in Paul's argument in Romans the response of faith(fulness) is much more closely bound up with the experience of persecution and the prospect of death than is commonly supposed.

So we have an analogy in a hybrid Jewish-Christian apocalyptic text that speaks of wrath against Israel first and then eventually against Rome, when two groups will be differently rewarded. On the one hand, those from all the nations who have endeavored to live piously and righteously—who have in effect done the *work* of the Law—will receive an imperishable prize of the peace that will follow the overthrow of Rome; on the other, a uniquely qualified group of those who have suffered for the sake of the covenant in the course of this historical transition will receive a crown of immortality.[5] My suggestion is that the tension between a judgment according to works and a justification by faith in Romans is to be resolved according to a narrative of this sort. The coming day of wrath will be a righteous and impartial judgment of the nations (including Israel) that will mean, in concrete social terms, "tribulation and distress" for everyone who does evil and "glory and honor and peace" for everyone who does good. But for those who, as we shall see, are called to live in the world *now* as agents of the impending eschatological transformation and who, therefore, are bound to suffer as Jesus suffered, faith(fulness) becomes the decisive criterion of survival and success.

---

5. Cf. *Mart. Pol.* 19.2: "By his endurance he overcame the unrighteous ruler, and thus gained the crown of immortality . . ."

6

Israel Will Not Be Saved by Works of the Law

It has become clear enough that Paul's "gospel" in Romans cannot be explained adequately by reference to a personal narrative of sin and salvation, judgment and justification. It is, in the first place, the announcement to the *oikoumenē* that the God of Israel is about to vindicate himself in the eyes of the world by judging the dominant culture of Greco-Roman paganism through the one to whom he has given the nations as an inheritance. This is not a *final* judgment, which is why social, political, and religious outcomes matter. Those whose lives have been shaped by the narrative of Romans 1:19–32 will "perish": they belong to a world that is passing away. Those who persist in doing good in the hope of gaining glory and honor and immortality will attain the life of the age that will come after judgment. Because the behavior of the Jew, despite his inveterate presumption of religious and moral superiority, is no better than the behavior of the pagan, he will find himself—much to his shame—subject to the same condemnation.

So Paul now turns to address explicitly those who go by the name of "Jew"—let us imagine them gathered indignantly at the front of the motley crowd, eager to protest at his outrageous and deeply offensive claim that their God is about to judge the secrets of men *by the martyr Jesus*. He jabs his finger at them angrily. You are in possession of the Law, you have been instructed in the Law, you boast in the Law, but you *transgress* the Law—you are no better than your pagan neighbors, your vaunted circumcision might as well be uncircumcision, and as a result "the name of God is held in contempt among the nations because of you"! In fact, he warns, you may find the tables turned. You set yourselves up as "a guide of the blind, a light of those in darkness, an instructor of foolish ones, a teacher of children"; but you will be shown up as hypocrites by those Gentiles who by nature do the works that the Law requires. They will become *your* judges.

The issue here, Paul maintains, is whether the claim can be put forward with integrity that the God of Israel will judge the world that he previously handed over to moral debasement. The Jews were entrusted with the "oracles of God" for the sake of the whole world—they should indeed have been guides to the blind, a light to those in darkness, instructors of the foolish, teachers of children. But the implication is that Israel must be held accountable first. It is obvious to Paul's mind that the Jews have not been faithful with regard to what was entrusted to them. In the first place, they demonstrated their unfaithfulness at the very moment when the Law was given to them by exchanging the truth of God for a lie and worshipping the image of a calf. Then in more general terms Scripture makes it clear—Paul cites the evidence in 3:10–18—that they are as much under the power of sin as the Greeks. That being the case, they have to face up to the fact that God will judge Israel first as a prelude to, and as a precondition of, judgment of the whole pagan world. The Law speaks first to Israel so that the mouth of wickedness in Israel may be stopped; and on that basis the whole world will be held accountable to God (3:19). Here is the theological rationale behind the argument that first the Jew and then the Greek will be subject to the wrath of God on a day of wrath. Paul has found in the resurrection of Jesus a compelling reason to believe that *in a foreseeable future* the derided and politically contained God of Israel will judge or overturn the pagan system that opposes and oppresses his people. But he cannot be *righteous* in doing that without first holding Israel accountable for its long history of unfaithfulness. Or to put it in historical terms, the eventual victory of YHWH over the gods, of Christ over Caesar, will not happen without the war against Rome and its protracted aftermath.

If You Are Named a Jew: 2:17–29

Paul now brings the problem of Israel sharply into focus. The nations are by definition *lawless*, and on the day of wrath they will be judged accordingly. The situation of the person who calls himself a Jew, however, is different. He may quite legitimately claim to "rely on the Law," "boast in God," be "instructed from the Law" so as to "know his will" and differentiate rightly between good and evil, be a "guide (*hodēgon*) to the blind," a "light to those who are in darkness," a teacher of those who lack wisdom because the law is the "embodiment of knowledge and of truth" (Rom 2:17–20). This is the Jew who understands that the Law has been given to Israel not for its own benefit only, but in some sense for the sake of the nations. The thought is widespread in contemporary Jewish writings and would have been familiar to—perhaps taken for granted by—the hapless hypothetical fellow whom Paul has accosted here. Wisdom of Solomon condemns the Egyptians for having imprisoned in darkness the sons of Israel "through whom the incorruptible light of the law was to be given to the age" (Wis 18:4). The grandson of Ben Sirach argues in his prologue to his grandfather's work that Jews who have received "education and wisdom" through the Law and the Prophets and the other ancestral writings are in a position to benefit "those outside." Indeed, his grandfather was led to "compose something pertaining to education and wisdom in order that lovers of learning . . . might gain much more in living by the law" (Prologue to Ben Sirach 12–14). *Sibylline Oracles* predicts a time during the hegemony of the Greeks when "the people of the great God will again be strong who will be guides (*kathodēgoi*) in life for all mortals" (*Sib. Or.* 3.194–95). *Testament of Levi* warns impious Israelites that they will bring a curse on the nation, "because you want to destroy the light of the Law which was granted to you for the enlightenment of every man" (*T. Levi* 14.4). Josephus boasts in his defense of Judaism against the accusations made by Apion that such is the excellence of the Jewish Law that "we are become the teachers of other men" (Josephus *Ag. Ap.* 2.293).

If the scattered communities of diaspora Judaism had actually lived up to the standards of the Law that was taught with such chauvinistic fervor in their synagogues, they might indeed have been a blessing to the nations, and the *oikoumenē* might have been a very different place. Idolatry might have been curtailed, immorality and injustice might have been mitigated, and the wrath of God might have been averted. Then their circumcision would have been something to boast about. But the sad fact was that the Jews extolled the virtues of a Law that denounced idolatry and prohibited adultery and theft—these three transgressions epitomize exactly the anti-pagan polemic of Romans 1:19–32—and then are caught stealing, fornicating, and robbing temples. They make a mockery of their God. As it was with the generation of the exile, "The name of God is blasphemed among the Gentiles because of you" (Rom 2:24; cf. Isa 52:3–5; Ezek 36:20–23; Dan 9:16). This is the intolerable irony that Paul thrusts in their faces—that the God of his people, despite extravagant biblical claims for his universal sovereignty, was regarded throughout the Greco-Roman world as a deity of little geopolitical significance, an impotent national god of dubious moral standing, represented by a troublesome and hypocritical people.

On the day of wrath, therefore—let us suppose, on the day when they hear report that Jerusalem has been "surrounded by armies" and realize that "its desolation has come near" (Luke 21:20)—they will find that their circumcision, their distinctive Jewishness, counts for nothing. It will not halt the Roman armies; it will not prevent the destruction and slaughter; it will not forestall the pillaging of Israel's wealth and the very public humiliation of captive Jews led in procession through the streets of Rome. Nor will it safeguard the Jews of the diaspora. Josephus has king Agrippa warn the militants in Jerusalem that by provoking war they endanger Jews across the *oikoumenē*: "for there is not a people in the world which does not contain a portion of our race. All these, if you go to war, will be butchered by your adversaries, and through the folly of a handful of men every city will be drenched with Jewish blood" (Josephus *J.W.* 2.398–99, LCL). So their circumcision will have become, in effect, uncircumcision—practically and historically ineffectual (Rom 2:25). It is a thoroughly realistic argument that is prefigured in Jeremiah's warning that physical circumcision alone will not preserve Israel from the wrath of God: "Circumcise yourselves to the Lord; remove the foreskin of your hearts, O men of Judah and inhabitants of Jerusalem; lest my wrath go forth like fire, and burn with none to quench it, because of the evil of your deeds" (Jer 4:4; cf. 9:25–26; Deut 10:16). The prophet envisages a time when invaders will come and besiege the cities of Judah (Jer 4:16), when "death has come up into our windows; it has entered our palaces, cutting off the children from the streets and the young men from the squares" and the "dead bodies of men shall fall like dung upon the open field . . ." (Jer 9:21–22). What will safeguard the status and integrity of Israel in this basic *historical and eschatological* sense will be the inward circumcision of

Gentiles righteousness used as judgment against Jews

the heart that will lead to the abandonment of evil deeds and a determination to practice "love, justice, and righteousness in the earth," in which the Lord delights.

If circumcision may become uncircumcision, however, there is a corresponding sense in which uncircumcision may become circumcision. If the non-Jew does what the Law requires, he will find on this day of wrath, when the world is turned upside down, that he is in the position of the righteous circumcised—he will be "justified" (Rom 2:13); his uncircumcision will be reckoned as circumcision (2:26); and in Paul's apocalyptically conceived trial scene, he will stand in judgment over unrighteous Israel (2:27). The Jews will be put to shame by righteous, God-fearing Gentiles. In his denunciation of a skeptical "evil and adulterous generation," Jesus argued that both the men of Nineveh and the Queen of the South would rise up at the judgment of Israel and condemn it. The point here is not that these righteous Gentiles are to be counted as part of the people of God or called "Jew" because they are inwardly circumcised.[1] Their significance within the eschatological scenario lies only in the fact that (unwittingly) they keep the precepts of the Law and, therefore, constitute a benchmark against which Israel will be judged. The argument about the authentic "Jew" is directed against the *Jewish* misconception that a circumcision that is visible in the flesh will be enough to save them from destruction. Only a circumcision of the heart, arising out of the renewal of God's covenant with Israel (cf. Jer 31:31–34; 32:40; Ezek 36:26–27), will secure a future for the people of God.

How Shall God Judge the World? 3:1–8

If it is the case, however, that circumcision of the flesh will be of no use to Israel on the day of God's wrath, that Jews will be hauled—metaphorically speaking—into the dock alongside unclean Gentiles to be judged by an *impartial* God, and, indeed, that righteous Gentiles, despite being lawless and uncircumcised, will stand in judgment over this evil and adulterous generation, the question is bound to be asked, perhaps by an understandably aggrieved disputant, whether the Jew has any advantage at all over the Gentile (3:1). What *more* (*to perisson*) does the Jew have than the Gentile? What is the value of the circumcision that so pointedly distin-

---

1. Against Wright, *Romans*, 448.

guishes him from his neighbors? Paul's answer is that the Jews indeed have something of enormous religious significance that the nations do not have—they have been "entrusted with the oracles of God." This is the only place in Paul's letters where the word "oracles" (*logia*) occurs. It is used in the Greek Old Testament for the "sayings" of God, notably in Psalm 118 LXX (= Ps 119); in Stephen's speech it is used for the Law that was given by angels to Moses (Acts 7:38).[2] But it also has strong pagan connotations (cf. the oracles of Delphi), which may hint at the thought that the Jews were entrusted with the word of God for the sake of the whole world.

Israel was "entrusted" (*episteuthēsan*) with the oracles of God but some proved to be "untrustworthy" or "faithless" (*ēpistēsan*). Where does that leave God? The vigorous diatribe style—the chaotic recollection of heated accusations and rejoinders—has left the line of thought badly fractured, but the point that Paul needs to make is that the *unrighteousness* of Israel does not fundamentally call into question the *righteousness* or rightness of Israel's God. On the contrary, it is precisely in his response to the unrighteousness of Israel that he is shown most clearly to be in the right. This is David's insight. By his admission that his "lawless deed" with respect to Bathsheba was a sin against God alone he shows that God is justified in his words, that he is victorious when he is judged (*en tō krinesthai se*: Rom 3:4; cf. Ps 50:6 LXX). The force of this assertion can be inferred from Psalm 108:6–7 LXX, where David records the words of those who have spoken deceitfully against him: "Appoint a wicked man against him; let an accuser stand at his right hand. When he is tried (*en tō krinesthai auton*), let him come forth guilty." It is also a central theme of the *Psalms of Solomon* that God must be shown to be right or justified in his judgment of unrighteous Israel. God has allowed the Gentiles to despoil Jerusalem, but the psalmist "shall prove you right, O God, in uprightness of heart; for your judgments are right, O God," because through this disastrous turn of events God has repaid the "sinners according to their actions (*kata ta erga autōn*), and according to their extremely wicked sins" (*Pss. Sol.* 2.15–16; cf. 3:5; 4:8; 8:26). Similarly, Israel was scattered among the nations so that "your righteousness might be proven right, O God, in our lawless actions. For you are a righteous judge over all the peoples of the earth" (*Pss. Sol.* 9.2). This is very close to Paul's argument. God is not merely *justified* in

2. Also Heb 5:12; 1 Pet 4:11.

inflicting wrath on unrighteous Israel ("*our* unrighteousness"); it is the necessary precondition for YHWH to act credibly as judge of the whole world (Rom 3:6).

This is a critical point. Paul's gospel—in the context of the argument in Romans—is that Jesus has been appointed Son of God in power through his resurrection from the dead. This is not a supra-historical affirmation: it has in view a historical narrative that will culminate in a judgment of the *oikoumenē* and the subjection of the political-religious enemies of the people of God to Christ (cf. 1 Cor 15:25; 2 Thess 1:7–10; 2:8). But if the marginal God of Israel is to overturn the status quo and judge the idolatrous and unrighteous pagan world, he is bound first to judge idolatrous and unrighteous Israel. At this point, as Paul rehearses in his mind the countless synagogue debates, he cannot help but hear the intrusive voice of a scandalized Jew who has failed to grasp the fact that the integrity—indeed, the righteousness—of God is at stake, and who raises the facetious objection that Israel might as well "do evil that good may come." Paul will return to this niggling complaint from a slightly different angle in chapter 6, but for now he merely brushes it aside and sets about cataloguing the evidence *from the Law* that the Jews are as much under the power of sin as the Greeks.

None Is Righteous, Not Even One: 3:9–20

The Old Testament texts that Paul quotes in Romans 3:10–18 speak not of a universal condition of sinfulness but of corruption and unrighteousness *in Israel*. They describe the powerful and corrupt who have led Israel astray, exploited the people, and oppressed the poor (Ps 14); the "bloodthirsty and deceitful" men who have rebelled against YHWH and who will be cast out "because of the abundance of their transgressions" (Ps 5); the "violent men, who plan evil things in their heart and stir up wars continually" (Ps 140); the arrogant and greedy who "hotly pursue the poor" and murder the innocent (Ps 10); the unrighteous whose "iniquities have made a separation between you and your God" (Isa 59:1–8); the wicked man who "flatters himself in his own eyes that his iniquity cannot be found out and hated" (Ps 36). At the same time, these texts speak of YHWH providing refuge for the poor, delivering the downtrodden, judging the wicked, defeating the enemies of his people, and establishing righteousness in Israel. When the Lord sees the extent of wickedness in Israel, he will put on justice against the wicked as a breastplate, deliverance of the poor as a helmet, vengeance against his enemies as clothing, and zeal for his people as a cloak; he will repay wrath to his adversaries according to their deeds; he will come to Zion to redeem his people from transgression (Isa 59:17–20). This full narrative should be kept in view, but the immediate point is that the Law itself exposes the deeply ingrained sinfulness of Israel. Whether or not the Jews continue to perform the "works of the Law," it is the knowledge of sin that will ultimately prove determinative for Israel's fate. So the mouth of the wicked is stopped (cf. Ps 63:11; 107:39–42); Israel is held accountable; and as a consequence the whole world may become "liable to judgment" (*hypodikos*).

Paul alludes in 3:20 to David's prayer that God might "not enter into judgment with your slave, because no one living will be counted righteous before him" (Ps 142:2 LXX). In the context of his argument it is likely that the substitution of "all flesh" (*pasa sarx*) for "every living person" (*pas zōn*) is meant to highlight the special significance of the statement for rebellious Israel according to the sinful flesh (cf. Rom 7:5, 18, 25; 8:3–8; 9:3)—we will reflect further on this nuance when we come to consider the statement in 8:3 that God sent his Son "in the likeness of sinful flesh." In any case, it is Israel that has the Law and that will, therefore, not be justified by "works of the Law."[3]

This has been Paul's charge throughout: the Jews have not lived up to the standards of the Law that should have made them a benchmark of righteousness in the world, a light to the nations. That same Law, therefore, has turned and bitten them. The Jews now stand in the way of God's judgment of the *oikoumenē* and must themselves first be held accountable in order that the "whole world may be held accountable to God." The distinction, therefore, between "works of the Law" and "faith," as Paul constructs it in Romans, cannot be mapped on to a largely abstract debate about how covenant membership is defined. It belongs, rather, quite specifically to an eschatological narrative about the imperiled existence of the people of God during a crisis of divine judgment: no Jew now will be justified on the day of wrath by "works of the Law" because the Law has consigned Torah-based Israel to destruction; so a way of existing must be

---

3. "All flesh" refers to Israel (cf. Matt 24:22; Mark 13:20; Acts 2:17). Also in particular Gal 2:15–16, where the restriction of the argument to Israel is clearer.

found that bypasses the Law, and a new benchmark must be established, on the basis of which the God of Israel will assert his claim over the whole earth.

7

The Justification of Israel, in the First Place, through the Faithfulness of Jesus

As we approach the pivotal argument about the "righteousness of God" in Romans 3:21–26, we should keep in mind that from the beginning of chapter 2 we have been listening to Paul address the Jew who boasts in the Law yet routinely transgresses against it, and who by his behavior brings the God of Israel into disrepute amongst the nations. Under these circumstances, Paul warns, the Jew is likely to find himself put to shame on the day of God's wrath by decent men and women in the pagan world outside the synagogue who *in effect* keep the precepts of the Law—who do not steal or commit adultery or rob temples. What the Jews have not understood in their moral and spiritual complacency is that Israel must be held accountable for its unrighteousness if the *God of Israel* is to judge the whole world.

That Paul now reiterates his earlier assertion that the righteousness of God has been made known reminds us that his thought is still controlled by Habakkuk's aphorism: in the gospel—in the outrageous claim that God has made Jesus heir to the nations—"the righteousness of God is revealed from faith for faith, as it is written, 'The righteous shall live by faith'" (1:17). The allusion invokes a parallel narrative of judgment and salvation by which the present circumstances are implicitly interpreted. First, Habakkuk is dismayed that flagrant injustice in Israel should have gone unpunished for so long: he is surrounded by violence and the perversion of justice, yet God does nothing (Hab 1:2–4). So too Paul states that previous sins have been "allowed to go unpunished" in the tolerance of God, but that the eventual vindication of God has now at last been made known; indeed, as will become clear, it has already been *anticipated* in current events (Rom 3:25–26a; cf. 2:4; Acts 14:16; 17:30). Secondly, Habakkuk is told that God will raise up the Chaldeans to punish unrighteous Israel but will not allow the merciless empire to go on destroying nations indefinitely. Paul, for his part, has argued that God is not unjust to "inflict wrath" on Israel because that is the precondition for judging the world (3:5–6). Thirdly, just as Habakkuk comes to the conviction that the righteous will survive on the day of wrath by trusting in God, Paul believes that representatives both of Israel and of the nations will be counted righteous on the day of wrath because of faith(fulness) and will live.

When Paul speaks of the "righteousness of God," what he has in mind is not an abstract ethical quality which might, for example, be imputed or transferred to the unrighteous, but divine action at critical moments in the history of his people, in keeping with contextually appropriate commitments, interpreted with reference to paradigmatic biblical narratives, by which the God of Israel is publicly vindicated, shown to be in the right. Isaiah 51:1–8 LXX speaks of God's "righteousness" as his active response to the crisis of Israel's rebellion and humiliation. Those who seek deliverance for Israel are urged to look to Abraham and remember God's re-creative promise to bless him and make him fruitful and multiply his descendants; God will restore the "waste places" of Jerusalem; they will become like the "garden of the Lord." Israel will be saved from the consequences of judgment, and through that salvation the "justice" of God will be established as a "light for the nations." The "righteousness" of YHWH quickly draws near: "my salvation will go out as a light, and on my arm nations will hope" (51:5; cf. 46:12–13; 59:16–18). So a people that knows the Law of God has no need to fear the reproach and contempt of the nations; their hostility will not last, but the righteousness of God will be forever and his salvation for generations of generations.

The Faithfulness of Jesus: 3:21–22

The eventual vindication of Israel's God is concretely and realistically preempted not only in the resurrection, by which Jesus was appointed to a position of authority with regard to the nations, but also in the obedience that took him to the cross, which in Paul's argument here is summed up in the phrase "through the faithfulness of Jesus Christ" (*dia pisteōs Iēsou Christou*, 3:22, my translation). There has been prodigious debate over the meaning of this phrase. I regard this translation as preferable to the conventional alternative "through faith in Jesus Christ," for reasons that I will outline, though in the end, given the narrative setting, the differences for interpretation may be slight.

In the first place, to the extent that the argument about righteousness and faith(fulness) in these chapters is shaped by Habakkuk's narrative about the wrath of God, we may suppose that what Paul has in mind is a *radical trust under conditions of eschatological turmoil*. It is not enough to say, as Francis Watson does, that faith "has its correlate in social practice."[1] It is rather a determination not to give in to fear or despair but, in effect, to trust that God will not allow the righteous in Israel to be destroyed along with the wicked. The phrase "obedience of faith" by which Paul defines the object of his apostolic calling suggests that he has in mind at least a belief that must be worked out in a distinctive and eschatologically relevant practice (Rom 1:5). He celebrates the fact that their "faith is proclaimed in all the world" (1:8), but it is apparent from 1 Thessalonians 1:8–10 that this faith presupposes precisely the eschatological narrative that emerges from Romans 1:19—2:16: it is a faith demonstrated in the fact that the Thessalonians, who have already experienced severe opposition (cf. 1 Thess 2:14), have abandoned the worship of idols and now wait for the resurrected Son who "delivers us from the wrath to come." This in itself does not preclude the sense "through faith in Jesus Christ," which is still to be exercised under difficult eschatological conditions; but the renewed conjunction of righteousness and faith in 3:21–22 reminds us that this is still essentially an eschatological argument and that faith is relevant because it is a substantive and lived-out response to extreme circumstances. In the end, one way or another, it is a matter of people trusting in the precedent of Jesus's practical faithfulness.

Secondly, the phrase "for all who believe" (*eis pantas tous pisteuontas*) would appear to be redundant if *dia pisteōs Iēsou Christou* is taken to mean "through faith in Jesus Christ." Does it really make sense to say, in effect, that the "righteousness of God" is both "*through* belief in Jesus Christ" and "*for* all those who believe" in him? The same problem arises in Galatians 2:16. We Jews, Paul argues, know that a person is not justified

1. Watson, *Paul*, 231.

by works of the Law but *dia pisteōs Iēsou Christou*; indeed, he says, we believed in (*eis*) Christ Jesus *in order that* we might be justified *ek pisteōs Christou* and not by works of the Law, because by works of the Law no flesh will be justified. The end and the means to the end are effectively the same if the noun and the verb have the same referent. Moreover, by differentiating between the *pistis* of Jesus and the *pistis* of those who are justified "through the redemption that is in Christ Jesus" (3:24) we provide ourselves with a cogent explanation of the statement in 1:17 that in the gospel the "righteousness of God is revealed from faith for faith."[2]

This move may avoid the redundancy, but it raises the question of whether a legitimate semantic distinction can be made between the noun *pistis* for the "faithfulness" of Jesus and the verb *pisteuō* for the act of believing. Watson objects, on the one hand, that the influence of Habakkuk 2:4 on references to faith in this passage makes it "difficult to argue that some refer to the faithfulness of Jesus, others to the faith of the contemporary believer";[3] and on the other, that the distinction in Pauline usage is largely attributable to a pattern of scriptural citation (e.g., Gen 15:6 in Rom 4:3 and Isa 28:16 in Rom 9:33), where the evidence suggests, in fact, that the verb and the noun are interchangeable.[4] But it is the case, nevertheless, that a general semantic distinction exists—and is readily illustrated from the Septuagint and New Testament—between a *pistis* that is directed towards an object such as God or a promise and a *pistis* that is itself the object of trust, denoting the quality of "faithfulness" or "reliability," or an object given as a proof or pledge. This distinction is not found in the verb: *pisteuō* does not have the corresponding sense of "to be faithful," which is why we do not find Jesus as the subject of the verb in Paul.[5] So where the subject is clearly the same, we would expect *pistis* and *pisteuō* to have the same meaning, determined by the verb: for example, Abraham "believed" and his "belief" was reckoned as righteousness (Rom 4:3, 5). In 3:22, however, the subject is not clearly the same—this is precisely the issue in dispute; and the problem of redundancy may then indeed make the subjective genitive more attractive.

---

2. Cf. Witherington and Hyatt, *Romans*, 101.

3. Watson, *Paul*, 239.

4. Watson, *Paul*, 240–43.

5. Against Esler, *Conflict and Identity*, 157.

Thirdly, we have two further prepositional *pistis* statements, also logically linked to the affirmation of God's righteousness, in 3:25–26 that lend support to this interpretation: God demonstrates his righteousness, first, by putting Jesus forward as an expiation *dia pisteōs* and, secondly, by justifying *ton ek pisteōs Iēsou*. To speak of God putting Jesus forward as an expiation *through the faith that people have (in Jesus)* makes little sense: *dia pisteōs* needs to refer to a concrete action or circumstance that has, in some way, demonstrated the righteousness of God. A parallel to the second phrase is found in Romans 4:16: the promise is guaranteed "not only to the adherent of the law (*tō ek tou nomou*) but also to the one who shares the faith of Abraham (*tō ek pisteōs Abraam*)." Clearly this does not mean "the one who has faith in Abraham"; rather, the faith that Abraham exhibited constitutes a seminal counterpart to the Law, with which others identify through their own faith ("who is the father of us all").[6] Admittedly, in this case *pistis* refers to Abraham's *belief* in the promise of God, not to his faithfulness; but this is because we have shifted between two narratives of faith, corresponding to the two senses of *pistis*—that of Habakkuk 2:4, which is *pistis* as "faithfulness" under eschatological stress, and that of Genesis 15:6, which is *pistis* as belief in the promise regarding the future of the people. But grammatically, the point stands: God justifies "the one from the faithfulness of Jesus"; the promise is guaranteed to "the one from the faith of Abraham."

My suggestion, therefore, is that the ambiguity that we find in the word *pistis* correlates with a narratively constructed distinction that lies at the heart of Paul's thinking about how God is shown to be righteous. The verb *pisteuō* is unambiguous: it denotes the act of believing or having faith in something or someone—such as Abraham believing in the promise of God or the saints in Rome believing in the redemptive significance of Jesus's death. The noun, however, can mean i) "belief/faith in" something or someone, or ii) "faithfulness," in the sense, for example, of Jesus's obedience to the point of death (cf. Phil 2:8) or of the saints' steadfastness in the face of persecution. In the context of Romans the first sense aligns with the story of Abraham: the *pistis* of Genesis 15:6 is paradigmatic for

6. Campbell, *Deliverance of God*, 643–44, points out that the argument that the subjective sense of *pistis Christou* would have been signaled by an arthrous construction is directly falsified by Rom 4:16 and Gal 2:20. He argues, further, that Apollonius's "rule" regarding genitive constructions "*indicates a subjective construal of the relevant genitive*" (645, Campbell's italics).

the belief or faith that the churches must have in the God who, against the odds, secures the future of his people—a theme which we will consider further in the next chapter. The second sense of "faithfulness" aligns with the narrative of Habakkuk: the *pistis* of Habakkuk 2:4 is paradigmatic for the "faithfulness"—both of Jesus and of those who follow him—by which the churches will survive the wrath of God.[7] Since in Romans 3:22 the argument is still essentially controlled by the Habakkuk paradigm, it is likely that *dia pisteōs Iēsou Christou* links the revelation of the righteousness of Israel's God with the story of Jesus's faithful suffering and obedience to the point of death—the narrow and difficult path leading to life apart from the broad way of Israel under the Law that would terminate in destruction (Matt 7:13–14). Indeed, it may be just the intertextual pressure from Habakkuk that accounts for the unusual construction here. In view of this it will at times be helpful to preserve the cumbersome ambiguity of "faith(fulness)": the *pistis* of the believer is both the "faithfulness" of Habakkuk 2:4 and the "belief" of Genesis 15:6.

If the concern is then raised that this appears to be pulling us in the direction of a proto-Arian Christology, as Philip Esler argues,[8] the response must be that it is precisely by way of the extreme *faithfulness* of Jesus, whose course runs directly counter to that of the hubristic ruler who first grasps at divinity but then is brought low, that we arrive at the acclamation of Jesus's lordship in the terms of Isaiah 45:23 (Phil 2:6–11).[9] We should not miss the fact, moreover, that Jesus is presented here expressly as a model to be emulated by a community that is suffering for the sake of Christ and must, therefore, if it is to survive, find the unity of mind and purpose which is theirs in Christ Jesus, "who, though he was in the form of God . . ." (Phil 1:29—2:6).

7. Against Campbell, *Deliverance of God*, 613–16, this does not require a *christological* reading of Habakkuk 2:4 as such. It is enough to suppose that Paul understands the general relevance of the saying and its narrative setting for interpreting, first, the "faithfulness" of Jesus and, secondly, the "faithfulness" of those who are following him.

8. Esler, *Conflict and Identity*, 158.

9. Note Campbell's important argument about the "underlying martyrological narrative" (Campbell, *Deliverance of God*, 647–56).

Redemption and Expiation: 3:24–25

As a way of faithfulness, however, "for all who believe" it may also be understood as a "redemption" and as an "expiation/propitiation" (3:24–25). Both terms presuppose a national rather than a personal narrative. These classic salvation texts cannot be detached from the overarching argument that if God is to overthrow the pagan world, he must first judge Israel, which raises the question of how some part of Israel may be rescued in advance of the destruction. Jewish usage does not fully explain the significance of Jesus's death, but we may identify nevertheless deep geological structures that have shaped the landscape through which the turbulent river of Paul's argument has cut its way.

First, it is unlikely that Paul intended the word *apolytrōsis* to evoke the "redemption" of the Israelites from slavery in Egypt.[10] His argument does not yet have the theme of liberation from slavery in view: that comes later, when he addresses the secondary question about remaining in sin (cf. 6:1–2).[11] Ben Witherington and Darlene Hyatt point out, "there are no OT quotations or really any convincing allusions to Exodus discussions of sacrifice and liberation."[12] The dilemma faced is not the Exodus one of slavery or freedom but the eschatological one of destruction or life—these constitute quite different paradigms. The narrative background, therefore, is more likely suggested by Hebrews 9:15: "a death has occurred that redeems (*eis apolytrōsin*) them from the transgressions committed under the first covenant" (cf. Eph 1:7; Col 1:14). The allusion is to the drama of the Day of Atonement, when the high priest offered sacrifice "for himself and for the unintentional sins (*agnoēmatōn*) of the people" (Heb 9:7). Jesus is depicted as the high priest of a second covenant who through his death entered the holy place and "obtained a redemption (*lytrōsin*) of the age" (9:12, my translation).

---

10. Against Dunn, *Romans 1–8*, 169; and Wright, *Romans*, 471.

11. Later Paul speaks of a liberation from the slavery of sin (e.g., Rom 6:16–22), but he uses *eleutheroō* rather than *(apo)lytrōsis* and cognates.

12. Witherington and Hyatt, *Romans*, 92–93; though conceivably the theme of Isaiah 51 is still playing in the background. The God who brought rescued and redeemed (*lelytrōmenois*) Israel from Egypt will bring back his people to Zion; the sorrow of oppression will be replaced by "praise and joy" (51:10–11 LXX; the sentence structure is rather different in the Hebrew).

The Justification of Israel, in the First Place, through the Faithfulness of Jesus

This redemption in Christ Jesus is had now *in anticipation of a future redemption* on a day when the disciples will raise their heads because their redemption is drawing near, when they will be vindicated along with the Son of Man for their witness against the corruption and faithlessness of the rulers in Jerusalem (Luke 21:27–28); when the "sons of God" who suffer with Jesus will receive the redemption of their bodies for which they wait (Rom 8:23). In Ephesians the saints have "redemption" through Jesus's blood, the forgiveness of their trespasses against the Law, but this anticipates a future "day of redemption"—an "evil day" when they will have to arm themselves against the "spiritual forces of evil in the heavenly places" in order to stand firm (Eph 1:7, 14; 4:30; 6:10–18; cf. Col 1:14).[13] The consistent anticipatory structure of Paul's thought emerges again: the eschatological argument is that believers have this redemption *now* because they will need it when the day of God's wrath comes.

Secondly, in the case of *hilastērion* the Day of Atonement setting is unequivocal. In the Septuagint the word mostly refers to the "mercy seat" that covered the ark of the covenant (cf. Exod 25:17–22). Paul's argument is that Jesus's faithfulness, culminating in his death, served a purpose analogous to the ritual on the Day of Atonement. Aaron is instructed to take the blood of the "goat of the sin offering that is for the people" and sprinkle it on and in front of the mercy seat; in this way he made "atonement for the Holy Place, because of the uncleannesses of the people of Israel and because of their transgressions, all their sins" (Lev 16:15–16). The underlying thought may indeed be that by its sins contemporary Israel has jeopardized the sanctity and security of the temple, and that Jesus's death has ensured the emergence of an alternative "Holy Place."[14]

13. The phrase "until redemption of the possession" in Eph 1:14 is difficult. Lincoln, *Ephesians*, 41–42, takes it to refer to the time when God will redeem his possession, that is, his people. It is likely that in Col 1:14 "redemption" belongs to a future moment when the saints, after a time of suffering when "all endurance and patience" will be required of them (1:12), will receive an "inheritance . . . in light." In 1 Cor 1:30 Paul states that God made Christ Jesus "our wisdom and our righteousness and sanctification and redemption." There is no explicit indication here of when this redemption is to take place, but it comes at the climax of a passage that predicts the destruction of the "wise" who merely pay lip-service to YHWH (cf. Isa 29:13–14, 20–21) and the salvation of the foolish and weak, the powerless and disenfranchised—the "poor" who will rejoice when justice is finally meted out to the lawless and arrogant (cf. Isa 29:19–20). Christ is for Paul the ground of the redemption that will come to the saints when the present age, the present form of the world, passes away (cf. 1 Cor 2:6; 7:31).

14. Note the two-part perspective of 1 John 2:2: "He is the propitiation (*hilasmos*) for

Thirdly, it is difficult not to hear echoes of the description of the suffering servant in Paul's argument in Romans 3–4.[15] But the servant suffers punishment (Isa 53:5) not for the sake of the world but because Israel has sinned: "stricken for the transgression of *my people*" (53:8). This is not a matter of personal sin; it is not a universal atonement. It is the widespread and persistent failing of national religious and moral life that brought the judgment of God upon the people in the shape of invasion, destruction, and exile. The personal transgressions of individual Jews are located and interpreted within this story. In his suffering the servant experiences the judgment of God against Israel; through his suffering many in Israel are accounted righteous; he bears their sins (53:10–12).

The restriction of the argument to the circumstances of first-century Israel, fourthly, is supported by the Theodotion text of Daniel 9:24, where the cognate verb *exilaskomai* is used for the atonement of the sins that have been responsible for Israel's state of protracted exile: "Seventy weeks were determined for your people and for your holy city for sin to be completed and to seal up sins and to expunge lawlessness and to make atonement for wrong-doings (*tou exilasasthai adikias*) and to bring in a righteousness of the age and to seal a vision and a prophet and to anoint the holy of holies" (my translation).

Fifthly, a story told in 2 Maccabees 12:39–45 helps us to reframe Paul's argument. Following a battle, Judas Maccabeus sent his men to recover the bodies of those who had fallen. They found concealed in the clothing of each of the dead "sacred tokens of the idols of Jamnia, which the law forbids the Judeans to wear." Understanding that this breach of the Law put them all at risk, they prayed to the Lord, the "righteous judge," that the sin might be blotted out. Judas took up an offering from among his soldiers and sent two thousand drachmas of silver to Jerusalem to provide for a sin offering (*peri hamartias thysian*). What principally motivated this action was the belief that those who had fallen asleep "in godliness" would be raised to receive the beautiful thank-offering that was stored away for them. The collection, therefore, constituted an "atonement (*exilasmon*) for the dead so that they might be delivered (*apolythēnai*) from their sin."

---

our sins, and not for ours only but also for the sins of the whole world."

15. Cf. Wright, *Romans*, 475–76.

The Justification of Israel, in the First Place, through the Faithfulness of Jesus

Finally, when the death of a faithful Jew is interpreted as an "expiation" in the context of an argument about judgment on Israel and the demonstration of the righteousness of God, we have to give consideration to the accounts in the Maccabean literature of the deaths of the righteous martyrs. The most important passage is 4 Maccabees 17:20–22: "And these who have been divinely sanctified are honored not only with this honor, but also in that, thanks to them, our enemies did not prevail over our nation; the tyrant was punished, and the homeland was purified, since they became, as it were, a ransom (*antipsychon*) for the sin of the nation. And through the blood of those pious people and the propitiatory of their death (*tou hilastēriou tou thanatou autōn*), divine Providence preserved Israel, though before it had been afflicted."

The death of the faithful martyrs—Eleazar, the seven brothers, and their mother—at the hands of Israel's enemy resulted in the liberation of Israel from tyranny, the punishment of the tyrant Antiochus, and the cleansing of the nation (cf. Lev 16:19): the language of the atonement is used to express the redemptive effect of their deaths *for the nation at a time of political and religious crisis*. Second Maccabees 7:37–38 reinforces the connection between the sacrificial death of the martyrs, who suffer because of Israel's sins (7:33), and the theme of the wrath of God against Israel: "I, like my brothers, give up body and life for our ancestral laws, appealing to God to show mercy soon to our nation and by torments and plagues to make you acknowledge that he alone is God and through me and my brothers to bring to an end the wrath of the Almighty that has justly fallen on our whole nation" (2 Macc 7:37–38). Theologically, this barely differs from Paul's argument in Romans: Jesus's death is a direct consequence or corollary of the wrath of God against sinful Israel; by means of it the sins of the people are forgiven, their enemies defeated, and their future secured. We should hear Paul speaking on behalf of Israel when he says that Jesus was "delivered up for *our* trespasses and raised for *our* justification": righteousness is reckoned to those who believe that the future of the people—not the eternal salvation of people in general—is guaranteed in this story of death and resurrection (Rom 4:25). The crucial difference, as we shall see, is that Jesus has suffered and been vindicated not in the course of the day of wrath but *in advance of it*, as a demonstration of God's intentions both to Israel and to the *oikoumenē*.

A Demonstration in the Present of a Vindication to Come: 3:25–26

In his disputes with the Jews Paul has argued that God cannot judge the pagan world without first judging Israel. They may appeal to their works of the Law, but the Law clearly informs those in the Law—that is, the Jews—that they are as much under the power of sin as the Greeks. Behind this is Paul's historically realistic conviction that it has come to the point that performing works specifically *according to the Law* will not avert the coming catastrophe, it will simply keep the Jews on a broad road that will sooner or later lead to destruction. However, an alternative scenario has emerged, outside the jurisdiction of the Jewish Law, by which God is shown to be just—not in an abstract sense but with regard to the quandary faced by those who seek to be righteous, who hope not to perish on the day of wrath. The Habakkuk narrative sets this within a temporal framework: the prophetic insight concerning the deliverance of the righteous comes *in advance of* the actual events through which the theological problems will be resolved. Similarly, the story of Jesus's faithfulness has disclosed the righteousness of God proleptically—in advance of the eventual day of judgment and vindication.

Although for theology generally the interpretation of the terms "redemption" and "expiation" has dominated discussion, it is important to note that Paul's argument in 3:25–26 is not simply that God put Jesus forward as an expiation but that God put him forward (parenthetically as an expiation through faithfulness) *as evidence or as a demonstration of his righteousness* (*eis endeixin tēs dikaiosynēs autou*). Jesus is God's response, in the first place, to the presumption on the part of Jews that they "will escape the judgment of God" because God has shown no interest in punishing former sins (cf. Rom 2:3).[16] Again, the argument is foreshadowed in Habakkuk's complaint that God does not intervene to rescue the victims of violence, that he is constantly confronted with appalling examples of Israel's iniquity, and that "the law is paralyzed, and justice never goes forth" (Hab 1:2–4). Habakkuk must simply wait and see, trusting that eventually YHWH will punish the wicked and deliver the righteous. Paul, however, can point to more concrete evidence of a coming resolution to

---

16. Cf. *1 En.* 13.2: "you will not be allowed forbearance (*anochē*) and supplication because of the unrighteousness which you have shown and because of all the works of impiety and wickedness and sin which you have taught to people."

the crisis of YHWH's impugned righteousness: the outcome has been anticipated in the story of Jesus. That this is also said to be a demonstration of God's righteousness "in the now time" (*en tō nyn kairō*) underlines the fact that there has been a theologically problematic delay in the execution of divine justice; but more importantly, it reinforces the point that the story of Jesus presages the future vindication *because*, as Paul explains in verse 26, God *will justify others on the basis of Jesus's faithfulness*. This is a crucial part of the eschatological argument. The eventual experience of the community on the day of wrath, at the climax to a long narrative of idolatry, immorality, wickedness, and postponed punishment, has been anticipated in the present period in the story of Jesus, who suffered at the hands of Israel's enemies, overcame death, and entered the life of the age to come. The argument of Romans 5–8 will show the extent to which the community itself is also written into this narrative about the eventual demonstration of the righteousness of God, but the point can be neatly illustrated from 2 Thessalonians 1:4–7: the endurance of the believing community under "persecutions and afflictions" is "evidence of the righteous judgment of God" (*endeigma tēs dikaias kriseōs tou theou*), which will be realized when he puts an end to their suffering and punishes their persecutors.

In the preemptive eschatological drama of Jesus's confrontation with both unrighteous Israel and the pagan oppressor, this attitude of resolute trust led to his arrest, ill-treatment, and execution. For this reason the faithfulness of Jesus is closely associated with his blood or his death, and we have the basis for regarding it also as an "expiation" or "propitiation" (the distinction between the two terms has little bearing on Paul's argument). But it should not be reduced to being merely an atoning *event*: it remains a lived-out response to the circumstances of this pressing eschatological moment, which is, therefore, also potentially the response of a community. As we heard from Paul at the outset, the righteousness of God has been revealed from *pistis* for *pistis*, from the faithfulness of Jesus for the faithfulness of those who have ventured to follow him (1:17); it has been made known through the *pistis* of Jesus Christ for the sake of all those who have *pistis* (3:22). If Jesus is the only "way" by which Israel might be saved from judgment (cf. John 14:6), this remains nevertheless a hollow prospect unless others take up their own cross and follow him.

In Paul's argument, therefore, justification is in the first place an eschatological category, in this specific sense: a pronouncement is made *with regard to a historical community* in anticipation of a day of wrath that threatens its very existence. When national Israel stands condemned by the Law to destruction because of persistent disobedience, to be declared righteous or to be justified is to have the hope of escaping that verdict and attaining to the life of the age to come. This is a corporate hope that defines a corporate trajectory, within which individuals, whether Jews or *incorporated* Gentiles (3:29–30), must find their own personal justification and peace with the Creator God.[17] On this basis they will be preserved when the day of God's wrath comes—first upon Israel, then upon the pagan world (cf. 5:9).

The God of the Gentiles Also: 3:27–31

The argument now switches between two different Old Testament typologies of the relationship between righteousness and faith. Up until this point the controlling paradigm has been Habakkuk's apocalyptic narrative: when the day of wrath comes and Israel's God is vindicated with respect both to unrighteous Israel and to the imperial aggressor, the righteous will live by "faithfulness," which is first the faithfulness of Jesus and secondly the faithfulness of the redeemed community. Indeed, the story of Jesus has been put forward in God's defense proleptically because it foreshadows the eventual story of the community, which will not perish but will find life on the day of wrath. But when Paul asserts in 3:28 that "we reckon (*logizometha*) a person to be justified by faith apart from works of the Law" (my translation), he has preempted the introduction of the second typology, which is given in the statement from Genesis 15:6 LXX that "Abram trusted God, and it was reckoned (*elogisthē*) to him as righteousness." There is no justification of the nations in Habakkuk, only of righteous Jews. But the story of Abraham's trust in the promise of God will allow Paul to include the nations in the argument about righteousness and faith. For if the God of Israel is one—to the jealous and at times

---

17. Against Moo, *Romans*, 28, who argues, against "scholars who have put 'people' questions" at the center that "The bulk of Romans focuses on how God has acted in Christ to bring the *individual* sinner into a new relationship with himself . . . , to provide for that *individual's* eternal life in glory. . . ."

ferocious exclusion of the gods of the nations—as Israel has heard (Deut 6:3–4, 14–15), he must also be God of the nations. The sovereignty latent in the confession is about to become a reality. By the inclusion of Gentiles in the people that has been justified in advance of the day when he will overthrow the pagan world, God signals his intention to be acknowledged by the nations; and the eschatological purpose is embodied in the very existence of a global community consisting of both the circumcised and the uncircumcised.

The justification of both Jews and Gentiles on the basis of faith does not mean that the Law has become irrelevant or ineffectual. On the contrary, it is precisely through the act of "faith" or "faithfulness" that the Law is made to stand. Two texts provide a suggestive interpretive background to the phrase "we make the law stand" (*nomon histanomen*). In 2 Kings 23:24 LXX Josiah "made the words of the Law stand (*stēsē*)" (my translation) by removing the sorcerers and idols from Judah and Jerusalem. In 1 Maccabees 14:29 Simon and his brothers resist Israel's enemies so that the "sanctuary and the law might be made to stand (*stathē*)" (my translation). This would lead us to think that Paul is not interested in maintaining the Law in the abstract sense or as a matter of principle. His point would be that by means of the action or stance of "faith" at this time of eschatological crisis the integrity of the covenant relationship is maintained in the face of both internal religious and moral corruption and external pressures to apostatize.

8

It Was Reckoned to Him as Righteousness

This would have been a well-known story . . . At the time of Antiochus
Epiphanes' brutal campaign to suppress Jewish religious practice (167
BC), a priest named Mattathias left Jerusalem, horrified by the defilement
of the city by the nations, and settled with his five sons in Modein. "Woe
to me," he lamented, "why was I born to see this, the destruction of my
people and the destruction of the holy city?" (1 Macc 2:7). When the king
sent his agents to Modein to enforce the apostasy, Mattathias refused to
comply: "If all the nations which are in the realm of the king obey him
so as to apostatize, each one from the religion of their fathers, and adopt
his commandments, both I and my sons and my brothers will walk in the
covenant of our fathers" (1 Macc 2:19–20). On an occasion when a citizen
came forward to perform the pagan sacrifice in accordance with the king's
edict, Mattathias killed both the Jew and the king's agent in a fit of rage,
and tore down the blasphemous altar. This act of intemperate piety signaled the beginning of the Maccabean revolt. Mattathias and his sons fled
to the mountains, and "many who were seeking righteousness and judgment (*dikaiosynēn kai krima*) descended to the wilderness to live there"
(1 Macc 2:29). The revolt quickly gathered momentum, strengthened by
an impromptu alliance with a powerful Hasidean group. In a program
of reactionary zeal that finds ready parallels in modern day narratives of
fundamentalist resurgence, they hunted down disloyal Jews, demolished
the pagan altars, forced the circumcision of all the uncircumcised boys
found within the borders of Israel, and successfully "reclaimed the law

out of the hands of the nations and out of the hands of the kings" (1 Macc 2:48).

Before he died, Mattathias spoke to his sons about the task that they faced. In a "time of destruction and fierce wrath" he urged them to be zealous for the Law and to give their lives "for the covenant of our fathers," to remember the "works (*erga*) of our fathers, which they did in their generations, and receive great glory and an everlasting name" (2:49–51); and he asked, "Was not Abraham found faithful (*heurethē pistos*) in testing, and it was reckoned to him as righteousness?"(2:52). Other examples of faithfulness to the covenant in the face of adversity are listed (notice that we have shifted towards the eschatological sense of *pistis* here): Joseph, Phineas, Joshua, Caleb, David, Elijah, Hananiah, Azariah, Mishael, and Daniel. Keep their example of loyalty to the Law in mind, he assured his sons, and "by it you will be glorified" (2:61–64).

What Is to Be Learned from the Example of Abraham? 4:1–8

Whether or not Paul had this particular account or related traditions in mind (cf. Ps 105:30–31 LXX; *Jub.* 30.17; 4QMMT C26–32), it helps us to reconstruct the general narrative shape of his argument about Abraham. For the writer of 1 Maccabees, Abraham provided the paramount archetype for righteous behavior under conditions of wrath: when tested by difficult circumstances,[1] he was found to be obedient to the commandment, and this faithfulness was reckoned to him as righteousness. So if Israel now is to survive the wrath that has come upon the nation because of impiety (cf. 1 Macc 3:8), they must trust in that example. Paul also foresees a coming day of wrath against Israel, similar in kind to the devastation and suffering inflicted by Antiochus Epiphanes but of much greater consequence.[2] Like the author of 1 Maccabees he attributes this to Jewish "impiety" (*asebeia*). Having just asserted that if God is to be God of Gentiles as well as Jews, justification must be "by faith apart from works of the Law" (Rom 3:28–30), Paul questions what there is to be *found* in—what is there to be learned from—the response of Abraham: "What then

1. Presumably the author has conflated Gen 15:6 and 22:1; see Kirk, *Unlocking Romans*, 64.

2. Kirk, *Unlocking Romans*, 64, sees the relevance of the parallel with 1 Maccabees but misses its full narrative significance.

shall we say? That we have found Abraham to be our forefather according to the flesh?" (my translation).[3] The sense of *heuriskō* is slightly different, but that is because Paul is asking his imagined Jewish auditors to judge *for themselves* what is to be made of the example of Abraham. If he was justified by works of the Law, then he would indeed be "our forefather according to the flesh"—because circumcision in the flesh, as an instance of obedience to the Law, would constitute a legitimate ground for boasting (cf. Gal 6:13). Then, to be sure, the sort of response to the crisis advocated by Mattathias or by the Qumran sectarians might be justified—the obstinate, and if necessary violent, refusal to permit compromise over observance of the Law, including the controversial "work" of circumcision. But that is not what the text says: Abraham was counted righteous not because he obeyed the commandment (that comes later), but because he believed the promise of God that his offspring would be as numerous as the stars of heaven. It is not emulation of the "works of the fathers" that will save Israel from the wrath of God but emulation of the response of faith(fulness), by which many sons will be brought to glory (cf. Rom 8:29–30; Heb 2:10). For the Jew who "works," who endeavors to adhere to the requirements of the Law, the outcome *under the present circumstances* will be "according to debt"—and because Israel's "works" have been evil, the nation will be repaid with destruction. But for the person who, *under the present circumstances*, believes that God will forgive the "ungodly" the outcome will be justification.

In an important respect, however, Abraham is of limited value as an archetype for Paul's argument.[4] He embodies a fundamental trust in the God who has made a promise about the future of his descendants; he models faith in the future of the people of God at a moment of uncertainty, when the future looks extremely insecure. But he can hardly be regarded as a model of "impiety." Paul must expand the argument if he is to show how *impious and unrighteous* Israel—and subsequently impious and unrighteous Gentiles—are also justified by faith. To this end he quotes from Psalm 31 LXX (= Ps 32). David admits to having acted lawlessly and impiously (31:5). For some time he has kept silent about his sin, but the burden of guilt has become intolerable; he therefore declares

3. The translation has its modern origins in Hays, *Echoes*, 54–55; see also Wright, *Romans*, 489–90; Kirk, *Unlocking Romans*, 60–61.

4. Contra Wright, *Justification*, 193.

his wrongdoing and so finds forgiveness: "Happy are those whose lawless behavior was forgiven and whose sins were covered over. Happy the man whose sin the Lord will not reckon..." (Ps 31:1–2 LXX). As a result he has the confidence that he will not be overwhelmed by affliction, the hostility of those who encircle him—the many "scourges of the sinner" (31:6–11). This allows Paul to correlate the positive reckoning of Abraham's belief in the promise as righteousness with the negatively framed affirmation that the person is blessed whose sin is not reckoned. So he arrives at a concise fusion of the two narratives: "to the one who . . . trusts in him who justifies the impious, his trust is reckoned as righteousness" (Rom 4:5, my translation). It speaks, on the one hand, of trust in the God who guarantees the future of his people, and on the other, of the certainty that this hope is open to the impious, whose lawless acts are forgiven, who would otherwise be subject to wrath.

Blessing and the Uncircumcision: 4:9–12

Up until this point the argument from the familiar *topos* of the justification of Abraham has been about *Jewish* righteousness.[5] This, Paul has claimed, is what *we Jews* should find in the story of "our forefather according to the flesh," augmented by the account of the forgiveness of impious David: an archetype of being counted righteous before God, even where there is a history of lawless acts, on the basis of a resolute trust in the God who guarantees the future of his people. This is a disturbing enough proposition for Jews who would instinctively cling to the Law when they felt threatened. But he now makes the profoundly disorienting connection with the question that was broached in 3:29–30: if God is one, as Israel has always proclaimed, must he not justify the nations in the same way that he justifies Israel? Abraham was found to be righteous—and in that respect blessed—*before* he was circumcised; and circumcision was explicitly instituted as part of a covenant between God and Abraham, in which God undertook to make him the father of a multitude of nations,

---

5. Against Wright, who argues that "we" in Rom 4:1 means "we *Christians*, Jews and Gentiles alike" (Wright, *Romans*, 489–90). Also Witherington and Hyatt, *Romans*, 15: "Abraham is called 'our Father' not because Gentiles were being integrated into Judaism through Jesus but because Abraham is the father of both Jews and the nations and so the forefather of a universal religion, and the nations are being integrated into the people of God via Jesus."

to give his descendants the land which he now inhabits as a "resident alien," and to be their God (Gen 17:4–8 LXX). For his part Abraham must be pleasing and blameless before God, and he and his male descendants must be circumcised "as a covenant sign (*sēmeiō*) between me and you" (Gen 17:1, 10–11 LXX). The cutting of the foreskin was a very tangible sign that this covenant would hold true for each successive generation. It was not simply an epitome of the whole Law or, for that matter, a boundary marker of the community. It was a sign of the promise, confirmation of a future integrity in the land under conditions that would eventually be elaborated as the Law of Moses; and Paul's argument is simply that the *future of the people of God*—that is, of the one who will be God of the whole world and not of Israel only—is no longer guaranteed by circumcision but is dependent entirely on the lived out faith(fulness) of those who have been called to be saints.

We have, therefore, two pathways leading from that seminal moment of trust in the promise of God. The first pathway consists of the "righteousness of faith" enshrined in the Law and embraced by a community of the Law; the second pathway consists of the "righteousness of faith" *apart from the Law*. Because, as Paul has been at pains to demonstrate from Scripture, the Law has produced wrath (4:15), the first pathway is coming to a devastating deadend. Behind this conviction is the argument that we find in a passage such as Deuteronomy 28:58–68. If the Jews are not "careful to do all the words of this law that are written in this book," then the Lord "will bring on you and your offspring (in LXX *spermatos* or 'seed') extraordinary afflictions, afflictions severe and lasting, and sicknesses grievous and lasting" (Deut 28:58–59). The promise to Abraham is explicitly negated: "Whereas you were as numerous as the stars of heaven, you shall be left few in number, because you did not obey the voice of the Lord your God" (28:62); just as before "the Lord took delight in doing you good and multiplying you, so the Lord will take delight in bringing ruin upon you and destroying you"; they shall be "driven away from the land to which you are going in order to inherit (*klēronomēsai*) it" (28:63, my translation). It has become clear, however, that an alternative pathway exists, independent of the Law and its ineluctable logic of transgression and wrath, accessible to both Jews and Gentiles, by which the original hope that the seed of Abraham would be "heir of the world" may be recovered.

Inheritance of the World: 4:13-25

According to the original promise Abraham would inherit the land of Canaan, and his seed would "inherit (*klēronomēsei*) the cities of their adversaries" (Gen 15:7; 22:17; cf. 28:4 LXX, my translation), but Paul may have in mind a Jewish expansion of the biblical hope. Many of the texts that are commonly cited as evidence of a universal expectation refer to the "land" of Israel (e.g. *Jub.* 17.3; 22.14).[6] In *1 Enoch* 5.7, however, the reference is probably to the whole "earth," which the elect will inherit, because we later have the statement made by God that "all nations shall worship and bless me" (*1 En.* 10.21). *Jubilees* 32.18-19 restates the promise to Jacob in unequivocally global terms: "And there will be kings from you; they will rule everywhere that the tracks of mankind have been trod. And I shall give to your seed all of the land under heaven and they will rule in all nations as they have desired. And after this all of the earth will be gathered together and they will inherit it forever."

It is not so clear, however, that "post-biblical Judaism began to interpret such language in cosmic proportions," as Kirk argues, or that Paul was thinking, along similar lines, of the inheritance of a supra-mundane "world-to-come."[7] Nothing in the passages cited from *Jubilees*, Ben Sirach, and *1 Enoch* points to such a development of the inheritance motif. The future described in *1 Enoch*, for example, is idyllic, but it remains this-worldly and falls short of the new creation described in Revelation 21, at least in the particular detail that death has not been finally destroyed (*1 En.* 5.10; cf. Isa 65:20). Two sections in *2 Baruch*, written after the destruction of Jerusalem, speak of a new and "undying world" that is promised to the righteous dead after they depart this life, whose appearance has been transformed following resurrection (*2 Bar.* 14.13 and 51.1-3). But this leads us into a quite different apocalyptic landscape. It has obvious

---

6. Cf. Dunn, *Romans 1-8*, 213. According to Sir 44:21 the inheritance of Abraham's seed would be from "sea to sea and from the river to the extremity of the land (*gēs*)." In Ps 71:8 LXX the phrase "from sea to sea and from river to the ends of the *oikoumenē*" describes the extent of divine sovereignty. It seems unlikely, however, that the same is intended in Sirach since he speaks in verse 23 of Jacob's inheritance as the division of the land among the twelve tribes. The promise originally referred to the land between the Nile and the Euphrates (Gen 15:18).

7. Kirk, *Unlocking Romans*, 67; Adams, *Constructing the World*, 167-71, argues that the inherited world is "to be the eschatological inheritance of God's elect, that is to say, the new or restored creation."

points of contact with Paul's theology, but there is no overt reference to the Abraham story and the specific promise that his seed would inherit the world. So at this point we should resist the pressure generated by later dogmatic developments to obfuscate the historical significance of Paul's argument for the sake of our post-biblical interest in a transcendent consummation.

In the context of Paul's argument in Romans, however, we must also reckon with the likelihood that the theme of judgment is in the foreground here. On the one hand, the promise that Abraham would be the "father of a multitude of nations" may have suggested to Paul's mind a connection with Psalm 2:8 LXX: "Ask of me, and I will give you nations as your inheritance (*klēronomian*), and the ends of the earth as your possession" (my translation). As we saw earlier, the significance of this allusion is not that Gentiles would be included in the people of God but that the nations would be judged and brought under the rule of Christ. On the other hand, it is specifically the world under judgment that has been in view in the argument about Jewish righteousness (Rom 3:6, 19). Paul shared the belief, therefore, with at least some strands of first-century apocalyptic Judaism—and had no doubt discussed this belief in the synagogues—that YHWH would soon assert his sovereignty over the nations, bring to an end the cultural and political hegemony of classical paganism, and give to his people the world as an inheritance. He might well have agreed with the writer of *Jubilees* that the descendants of Abraham would rule, quite literally, "everywhere that the tracks of mankind have been trod"—and if he did not imagine quite such an outcome, it is effectively what happened. But he would have disagreed strenuously regarding the conditions under which this radical historical shift would occur—not through works of the Law, but outside the jurisdiction of the Law, through the exercise of an active, historically grounded, faith(fulness).

The author of *4 Ezra*, also writing after the war against Rome, gives expression to Israel's thwarted hope of inheriting the world. He recounts the six days of creation, arguing that God had said that this world was created for Israel. He notes that according to Isaiah, in the eyes of God the nations are nothing, "they are like spittle" (Isa 40:15); yet "they domineer over us and devour us." The people of God, whom "you have called your first-born, only begotten, zealous for you, and most dear," have been given into their hands. So the despairing question is asked: "If the world has indeed been created for us, why do we not possess our world as an inheritance? How long will this be so?" (*4 Ezra* 6.55–59). Paul's gospel-argument is part of this conversation and directly answers the question: those who are descendants of Abraham on the strength of their eschatological faith(fulness) will inherit the nations when eventually God comes to judge and lay claim to the *oikoumenē*.

What characterizes the "faith" that was reckoned to Abraham as righteousness is its orientation towards a future existence.[8] It is faith in the God who "gives life to the dead and calls into existence the things that do not exist" (4:17). At one level, of course, it is Abraham whose body is as good as dead, and it is his offspring that do not yet exist (4:18–19). But this is again, in effect, a faith for faith, a faithfulness for faithfulness. The story is told, Paul argues, for the sake of those who now share the same confidence, expressed as the belief that God "raised from the dead Jesus our Lord, who was delivered up for our trespasses and raised for our justification" (4:24–25). The belief of this new hybrid community in the promise that the descendants of Abraham will inherit the world (in the mundane, historical sense that we have described) *will be counted* (*mellei logizesthai*) to them as righteousness when this day of judgment eventually comes. The suffering of Jesus as a consequence of Israel's sins and his resurrection constitute a decisive anticipation or preemption of the suffering and vindication of the community.

This, of course, has nothing to do with an *imputation* of righteousness—in the sense of the transference of an attribute from a person who has it to a person who does not have it.[9] Phineas was counted righteous because by slaying a Jew and his Midianite wife he made atonement for the people and averted the wrath of God (Num 25:6–13; Ps 106:30–31). For Mattathias Abraham was counted righteous because he remained faithful under testing; Jews who now remained faithful in defense of the covenant could likewise expect to be counted righteous and glorified. The Qumran sectarians are told that in the end time their obedience to the Law will be reckoned to them as righteousness "in that you have done

---

8. Kirk, *Unlocking Romans*, 64 correctly sees Abraham as a model of faithfulness rather than of a "punctiliar act of believing." Witherington and Hyatt write, "It is this remarkable faith, and not just any sort of faith, that was reckoned as righteousness—a faith that hoped against hope, a faith that in the time of testing did not give way to unbelief . . ." (*Romans*, 129).

9. Against, e.g., Piper, *Future*, 76–77, 168.

what is right and good before Him, to your own benefit and to that of Israel" (4QMMT C31–32). For Paul Abraham was counted righteous not because he performed works in accordance with or for the sake of the Law, but because he believed the promise of God. No mysterious soteriological transaction lies behind these "reckonings": the point is simply that the action or behavior is counted by God as a righteousness that will have a bearing on the fate of the people.

Simon Gathercole has argued that behind the language of reckoning as righteous, and behind the argument from Psalm 32:1–2 in particular, lies the thought of "heavenly books" in which a person's sins and righteous acts are recorded: "We can imagine a ledger for each person that records both sins and righteousness."[10] So when David is forgiven, the negative side of the ledger is "wiped clean," and he is therefore blessed. Since David is (supposedly) "without works," the positive side of the ledger is empty until God reckons righteousness to him—"that is, positive imputation!" There are a number of problems here. In the first place, Gathercole appears to have misread the "heavenly books" of *Jubilees* 30. The killing of the Shechemites by the two sons of Jacob is reckoned to them as righteousness and inscribed on the heavenly tablets as "blessing and righteousness . . . before the God of all" (*Jub.* 30.19). These tablets are a record of the "righteous" deeds of the sons of Jacob; they are not a ledger—there is no corresponding negative side on which their sins are listed. Instead there is a second book, a "book of those who will be destroyed," in which will be written the names of those who "transgress and act in all the ways of defilement" (30.22). Secondly, Paul does not say that the person of whom David speaks is "without works": the point is rather that a person is blessed "to whom God counts righteousness *apart from works (chōris ergōn)*." David is not without righteousness, it is just that a situation has arisen—God's patience with Israel has run out—in which justification can only come through faith(fulness), apart from works of the Law (cf. Rom 3:21). Thirdly, as Paul has constructed his argument, righteousness is not something that is simply and freely credited to a person who confesses that he or she has no righteousness on the basis of works. What he says is that when a person "believes in him who justifies the ungodly," that belief or faith is counted as a righteous act (4:5). As with Abraham, "righteous" is a divine judgment pronounced on *what a person does*. Paul insists that

---

10. Gathercole, *Boasting*, 247–48; see also Piper, *Future*, 168–69.

under the present eschatological conditions it will not be pronounced on works of the Law but on the work, so to speak, of trusting in the God who promised that the family of Abraham would inherit the world (4:13). This is a faith that *does* something.

In his debate with Piper over the nature of justification Wright insists that this is not an argument about "how people get justified." The question that Paul is working towards is rather, "Who are the family of Abraham?" Is this to remain essentially a family of Jews, with Gentiles perhaps welcomed at best as proselytes to Judaism? Or "might it actually be a family of *un*circumcised people, i.e. Gentiles, into whom Jews might struggle for admittance . . . ?"[11] Paul is not quite ready, as I think we will see later, to concede such a complete relativization of national Israel, but he is close, and Wright is certainly correct to read this as an argument about how God's purposes for his covenant people are fulfilled. But Paul's thought is still constrained by the eschatological premise. The point is not simply that Abraham believed before he was circumcised, thereby effectively giving the *uncircumcised* priority in the grand scheme of things; it is that he believed *in hope and against hope*, when the outcome was by no means assured; he believed when his own body was already "put to death"; he believed as an archetype for the sake of those, whether Jews or Gentiles, who in the now time have to trust that the one who raised Jesus from dead will likewise safeguard their future as individuals and as a community when the darkest forces of paganism conspire against them.

So having taken the Abraham detour in order to pick up the Gentiles, Paul now rejoins the main eschatological thoroughfare of his argument: when the day of wrath comes and all hell breaks loose, the righteous will live because they trust the antecedent of Jesus's suffering and resurrection and because, like Abraham, they believe that God will ensure the future of his people. Therefore, Paul can go on to say that those who have been justified by faith(fulness), in advance of the impending divine overthrow of the *oikoumenē*, not only have peace with God and so no reason to fear the coming distress; they have access to the grace that will enable them to stand "in the evil day" (cf. Eph 6:13–14); they boast in the hope of the glory of God that will be revealed to the world when this day comes, when at last the name of the God of Israel will be confessed among the nations; and they boast, too, in their afflictions (Rom 5:1–3), which, as we will now see, is by no means incidental to Paul's argument.

11. Wright, *Justification*, 191.

9

The Law of the Spirit of Life

It is time for a change of mood. Paul now speaks on behalf of those who have indeed been justified by their trust in the one who raised Jesus from the dead—those who are the concrete product of his message to both Jews and Gentiles that under conditions of "wrath" the "righteous shall live by faith" (Rom 1:16–18). He has in mind the beleaguered and insecure communities of saints that have sprung up in his footprints like fragile colonies of mushrooms from the spores of his improbable gospel, from Jerusalem to Illyricum—and no doubt he is also thinking of the saints in Rome. The argument is still a reminiscence of the circumstances of his active ministry, but the focus has shifted. The intention of God is to judge the ancient world—that is, in effect, to overthrow the régime of classical paganism and initiate a wholesale restructuring of the relationship between his people and the Greco-Roman *oikoumenē*. Judgment will begin with the Jews, who have shown themselves to be as much subject to the power of sin as the nations. A narrow path leading to life has been found apart from the Law—a way of faithfulness arising from Jesus's lived out and, we might say, *died out* confidence in the God who determines Israel's future; and this has become the basis for the hope of the community that when the day of wrath comes, the righteous will live by *their* faithfulness. But it has become painfully clear already to Paul and the churches that this will not be an easy journey to make: the sense of having been justified is only the starting point. So he begins to address the eschatological—that is, the dangerously and decisively transitional—situation of the communities of those who have left behind either the Law or the idols in order to serve the living and true God and are waiting for his Son from heaven, who will deliver them from the wrath to come (cf. 1 Thess 1:9–10).

It is noticeable that the argument of chapters 5–8 is much less reliant on Scripture: the imagined dialogue with the synagogues has given way to a conversation with groups that consist of Gentiles as well as Jews, and the rhetoric has changed accordingly. But it would be a mistake to suppose that the emphatic assertion that those justified by faith now have "peace with God" signals an irreversible move beyond the narrative about Israel into a realm of a dehistoricized faith.[1] These chapters still presuppose both the eschatological framework so carefully reconstructed in 1:16—4:25 from his disputes with the Jews and the overriding concern with the immediate fate of a people. Indeed, the existence of these new communities of faithfulness is integral to the argument about the revelation of the righteousness of God.

The Hope of the Glory of God: 5:1–5

The opening paragraph of this section (5:1–5) in many ways previews the climactic argument of chapter 8. Those who have been justified by faith have peace with God and may boast "in hope of the glory of God"; and Paul later writes that there is "now no condemnation for those who are in Christ Jesus" (8:1) and that "those whom he justified he also glorified" (8:30). The hope of glory cannot be separated from the rhetorically styled but nonetheless realistic process that leads from affliction to perseverance to approval and finally to a hope that "does not put us to shame"; in the same way the glory that will be revealed in the sons of God comes as the startling starburst against a night sky at the end of a long rocket trajectory of suffering (cf. 8:17–18). Finally, just as it is the love of God "poured into our hearts through the Holy Spirit" that underpins the transmutation of suffering into glory, so Paul will insist that no persecution will be able to "separate us from the love of God in Christ Jesus our Lord" (8:39). We should reckon with the fact, therefore, that the material of Romans

---

1. Witherington and Hyatt suggest that the paucity of OT allusions in chapters 5–8 points to the fact that Paul here "offers a sampling of his distinctive message to Gentiles" (Witherington and Hyatt, *Romans*, 20). This is unlikely: 5:10 speaks of *Israel* as enemies of God (cf. 11:28); 7:1 addresses those who know the Law; the argument about rebellion, Law and righteousness is in the background.

5:6—7:25 is bookended by this argument about the progression of the community from suffering to glory.

When Paul says that "we have peace with God," he means that they have been reconciled with the God who has revealed his intention to judge the idolatrous and unrighteous *oikoumenē*. Peace is the eschatological alternative to the "tribulation and distress," the destruction, that will come upon those who do evil (Rom 2:9–10); Israel has turned its back on God, choosing to walk a path of injustice, anger, and violence, and has not known "the way of peace" (3:10–18). In the Scriptures, peace is a natural concomitant of righteousness: God forgives the iniquity of his people, he withdraws his wrath, he restores the fortunes of Jacob, and "righteousness and peace kiss each other" (Ps 85:10). If Israel had paid attention to the commandments of God, "your peace would have been like a river, and your righteousness like the waves of the sea; your offspring would have been like the sand, and your descendants like its grains; their name would never be cut off or destroyed from before me" (Isa 48:18–19; cf. Ezek 37:26). It would be nice to think that Paul takes at least a passing subversive shot here at the Augustan ideal of Roman *pax* founded on Roman *iustitia*, but, frankly, this seems beyond the scope of his argument.[2]

That the community may "boast in hope of the glory of God" also has an eschatological fulfillment in view, though the thought can be taken in two directions. On the one hand, the point may be that *as the nucleus of a restored people of God* they have been convinced by the resurrection of Jesus that the glory of God will, in the foreseeable future, be revealed in the world through what he does in and for his people. If Witherington and Hyatt are correct in thinking that Jeremiah 9:23–24 lies behind Paul's statement,[3] then Israel should boast in the Lord who "practices steadfast love and judgment and righteousness in the land" because the days are coming when God will "scatter them among the nations whom neither they nor their fathers have known, and I will send the sword after them, until I have consumed them" (Jer 9:16). Isaiah speaks of the day when the Lord of hosts "will be the garland of hope, which is woven of glory, to what is left of my people" (Isa 28:5 LXX); he will "make the glory of his voice to be heard" when he defeats his enemies in his wrath (Isa 30:30

---

2. Against, e.g., Wright, *Romans*, 515.

3. Witherington and Hyatt, *Romans*, 135.

LXX); and when he brings his people back from exile "the glory of the Lord shall appear, and all flesh shall see the salvation of God" (Isa 40:5 LXX). On the other hand, given the emphasis on suffering in 5:3–4, Paul may anticipate here the argument of Romans 8 that those who share in Christ's sufferings and death will share in his glory.

In any case, Paul cannot boast in the hope of glory without at the same time boasting in the afflictions that both the apostles and the churches have had to endure. "Affliction" produces "perseverance," which leads to a "character" tested or approved by the ordeal of persecution (Paul uses *dokimē* to refer to the "testing" of affliction in 2 Cor 8:2), which finally provides the experiential basis for the "hope" of being saved from—that is, of surviving—the destruction of the day of wrath. It is a simple, focused, and very practical argument: through the sufferings of the present they will develop the qualities of character, and with that the confidence, that will enable them to endure the wrath that is to come. He is retelling a familiar Jewish story, of which the seven brothers' renowned defiance of Antiochus Epiphanes provides only the most striking example: "Therefore, tyrant, put us to the test, and if you take our lives because of piety, do not think that, by torturing, you hurt us. For we, through this suffering and endurance, shall gain the prizes accorded virtue and shall be with God, for whose sake we suffer . . ." (4 Macc 9:7–8). For Paul the premise and the context have shifted radically, but the sense of historical realism should be retained: it is the story of a community of faith struggling to overcome—in the present, not in some hypothetical future—a level of pagan hostility that is aimed at the suppression of its highly critical, unaccommodating witness to the one God.

What sustains the community under these conditions is the love of God, which has been "poured into our hearts through the Holy Spirit who has been given to us" (5:5). This is now the commonplace language of modern piety, and its eschatological cutting edge has been badly blunted. But the Spirit "poured out" on the day of Pentecost was the Spirit that would be given to form an egalitarian prophetic community within Israel—a community that would dream dreams and see visions of the calamitous day of the Lord that was coming and proclaim good news to those whom the Lord had called (Joel 3:1–5 LXX = 2:28–32). The church began as a movement that would call Jews to save themselves from a "crooked generation" that would soon be destroyed and to become part of a "new covenant" of life. Paul thinks of the diaspora churches in much the same way, except that their horizon has been expanded to encompass judgment not on Israel only but on an entire civilization.

While We Were Still sinners: 5:6–11

Paul continues to speak *on behalf of* scattered groups of Jews and Gentiles who have responded in similar fashion, and to similar effect, to the extraordinary story that he has told about the God of Israel. *We* are confident, he says, that we have already been declared righteous in advance of the day of God's wrath. But in order to arrive at that eventual historical vindication we have to follow Jesus down a narrow and difficult path of suffering. The argument that follows, through to the end of chapter 5, is intended to provide specific and direct support for his conviction that the community that has been justified proleptically through Christ and that has begun this journey will *in the end* arrive at a super-abundant life. Romans 5:6–21, therefore, is not a general account of salvation in Christ against the universal backdrop of Adam's sin; it is a bespoke argument, carefully tailored to meet the requirements of the specific eschatological narrative that is unfolding in the letter. This does not mean that it is without universal significance: a bespoke suit is not less a suit than one that has been bought off the rack. But if we are to respect the literary integrity of the text, we must give proper recognition to the contingency of the argument.

The basic point that Paul makes here is that those who know for a fact that they have been reconciled with God *in the present* (because in powerful ways they have experienced the *Spirit* of God) can be confident that they *will participate in a future life* beyond the day of God's wrath. This linking of present and future conforms to the emerging structure of Paul's argument about the entanglement of the people of God in a process that will culminate in the overthrow of the imposing edifice of the Greco-Roman *oikoumenē*, when not one stone will be left standing on another. What happened first in the story of Jesus is being appropriated, experienced, lived out, by a growing community of Jews and Gentiles *in anticipation of* the eventual day of accountability, when first Israel and then the *oikoumenē* will be judged. The churches recapitulate in their own existence, in the present time, the story of Jesus's suffering and vindication as a foreshadowing or guarantee of the future victory over pagan opposition and the public, *oikoumenē*-wide vindication of the family of Abraham—when, in the language of the story of the Son of Man community, those who have suffered with Jesus will be brought with him before the throne of the Ancient of Days to receive "dominion and glory and a kingdom" (Dan 7:14). We misunderstand Romans—indeed, we misunderstand the whole of the New Testament—if we fail to raise our eyes and notice the smoking, rumbling volcano of divine judgment looming ominously in the background, as Vesuvius overshadowed ill-fated Pompeii.

The case is made first in an argument about reconciliation with God in 5:6–11, and then by means of a negative analogy that contrasts the effect of Christ's *obedience* with the effect of Adam's *disobedience*. Paul identifies himself with Israel in transition when he says that at a critical moment in the narrative (*eti kata kairon*), when we were "weak," under judgment as a consequence of sin and at enmity with God, Christ died for the ungodly. The language continues to evoke, though less overtly and less precisely, a Jewish self-understanding shaped by a narrative of judgment and restoration. For example, the psalmist writes that the unrighteous in Israel are "sinners" and "enemies of the Lord"; they will perish, but the Lord "knows the ways of the blameless, and their heritage shall be forever; they shall not be put to shame in an evil time" (Ps 36:18–20 LXX). Hosea claims that Israel has been made "weak" by their iniquities (Hos 5:5; 14:2 LXX). If the Jews are enemies of God and threatened with calamity, they are in need of reconciliation (cf. Rom 5:9–11). Second Maccabees is written ostensibly as a letter from Jews in Jerusalem to their "brothers in Egypt" regarding the celebration of the purification of the temple and the defeat of the army of Nicanor, who had been sent by Ptolemy "to wipe out the whole race of Judea" (2 Macc 8:9). It opens with a prayer that God will bring peace, that he will be reconciled (*katallageiē*) to them and not forsake them "in a time of evil" (2 Macc 1:1–5). The ghastly torments inflicted by Antiochus on the seven brothers are interpreted as a sign of God's anger towards Israel: "we are suffering because of our own sins"; but they are confident that after this rebuke and disciplining "he will again be reconciled (*katallagēsetai*) with his own slaves" (2 Macc 7:32–33). Following the defeat of Nicanor, the army of Judas Maccabeus "implored the merciful Lord to be wholly reconciled (*katallagēnai*) with his slaves" (2 Macc 8:29).

This language—these texts and stories—was no doubt part of the ideological décor of the Jewish communities of the eastern empire, the belief system with which their collective mind was wallpapered. We are not always made directly aware of its presence in the background, and we cannot always be certain in what way and to what extent it is determinative for interpretation. But when a first-century Jew reconstructs for the benefit of his readers in Rome an argument that is the product of a passionately engaged dialogue with first-century Judaism, we have to assume that the multilayered and often contradictory discourse of first-century synagogue faith is presupposed and must somehow be reinstated if the argument is to be understood as originally intended.

The Life of the Age: 5:12–21

So Paul argues that if a people that was at enmity with God has been reconciled by Jesus's singular act of faithfulness, which is not an abstract and isolable salvation-historical event but a certain type of behavior under concrete social conditions, they have every reason to believe that they will be "saved by him from the wrath of God" (5:10). If God would do this for them when they were enemies, they may be certain that, when the time comes, he will deliver from destruction those with whom he has been reconciled.

Habakkuk's aphorism has already established that deliverance from destruction on a political-religious scale is a matter of life rather than death. In 5:12–14 the existential reality of death as the destructive power that ultimately undergirds the wrath of God is briefly and somewhat disjointedly set out. The analogical argument that begins in 5:12 is left hanging in mid-air like a half-finished bridge. The account of the entry of sin and death into the world has its antecedents in Jewish thought, which reminds us that Paul is still primarily in conversation with Judaism: "God created human beings for incorruption and made them the image of his own nature, but through the envy of the devil death entered the world, and those who belong to his party experience it" (Wis 2:23–24).

Paul is not greatly interested in either the biology or the metaphysics of the transmission of death. Adam sinned and death simply *entered* the world; and "inasmuch as" or "because"[4] all people sinned, death became

---

4. Dunn thinks that the classic debate over the meaning of *eph' hōi* has "more or less

a universal experience (5:12). He interrupts himself at this point in order to explain, parenthetically, that this immutable law of sin and death was in force even where there was no explicit commandment of God to be transgressed—people died because "sin was in the world." What changed with the introduction of the Law was that sin came to be "counted." Israel was not merely subject to the law of sin and death. Because like Adam it had the commandment, Israel was expressly accountable—and for this reason, as Paul has already argued, the world could be held accountable (cf. Rom 3:6, 19–20). Paul, therefore, distinguishes between a universal condition that prevails apart from the Law and a particular narrative of sin and judgment that is determined *by the Law*.[5] In different ways Adam is at the genesis of both situations: on the one hand, through this one man sin and then death entered the world, resulting in the death of all people; on the other, by transgressing the explicit commandment of God he prefigured Israel's transgression of the Law—and perhaps in that respect Adam, as one who received the commandment, is a type not of Christ but of Moses who is to come (5:14).[6]

The argument that Paul develops in Romans relates primarily to this second line of thought: it has to do with a final endplay for the Mosaic covenant and the protracted confrontation between an emerging church and a moribund paganism. We are reminded here that this narrative is nested within—and is a consequence of—a larger story that begins with Adam's deadly transgression and imagines an ultimate future when "the creation itself will be set free from its bondage to corruption" (Rom 8:21). But it is not quite correct to say, as Kirk does, "Paul argues for an Adamic rather than Mosaic source of condemnation at the final judgment."[7] It is the Law that will condemn Israel at an impending judgment because it brings knowledge of sin and accountability (1:32; 2:12, 25; 3:9–20)—an accountability, indeed, that may be extended indirectly to the whole world. But the reason Israel is condemned rather than justified by the Law is that it is as much subject to the power of sin as the rest of humanity because of

---

been settled in favor of the meaning 'for this reason, that' or 'in view of the fact that'" (Dunn, *Romans 1–8*, 273).

5. These are not merely two sides of the "human condition within the epoch of Adam" (Dunn, *Romans 1–8*, 275).

6. This understanding of *typos tou mellontos*, in many respects the more natural one, has support from Robinson and Scroggs (see Dunn, *Romans 1–8*, 277).

7. Kirk, *Unlocking Romans*, 106.

Adam. This is the point of the extensively used imagery of a captivity to the power of sin: it comes in the end as a shocking realization that the Law of God can only collude with and not overcome the brute anthropological reality of sin. The complex analogy between Israel's sin and Adam's sin that Paul develops in 7:7–25 in the form of an autobiographical narrative serves the same purpose.[8] Only the narrative of judgment and restoration, death and new life, destruction and new creation, of which the brief, intense story of Jesus's death and resurrection is the preface and synopsis, can change the fundamental given of sin and death.

So the argument here—whatever else we may find in the New Testament—is that God overcomes death not cosmically or for humanity in Adam but *for his people*. The reasoning can be exemplified, by way of a slight digression, from the classic statement about death in Isaiah 25:7–8: "And he will swallow up on this mountain the covering that is cast over all peoples, the veil that is spread over all nations. He will swallow up death forever . . ." On the face of it, this appears to speak of a universal defeat of death, but in context the thought may be constrained by the covenantal narrative. We are again misled by the translation of *'erets* as "earth" in Isaiah 24. It is not the *earth* but the *land* of Israel that is made desolate, defiled by its inhabitants—clearly not the peoples of the world but Jews who have "transgressed the laws, violated the statutes, broken the everlasting covenant" (24:5). It is the *land* that is devoured, in keeping with the terms of the covenant (Deut 28–30), by a "curse" (*'alah, ara*) of decay and death, most seriously in the form of military destruction. It is *Israel* that is left devastated *in the midst of the nations*, "as when an olive tree is beaten, as at the gleaning when the grape harvest is done" (24:6, 13). But then we have a characteristic reversal in the prophetic narrative: YHWH will punish the hosts of heaven and the kings of the earth that have laid waste to Jerusalem and Israel (24:21—25:2); and because Israel's God has been a stronghold to the poor and needy among his people, the nations will glorify and fear him (25:3–4). Then YHWH will take away *the* shroud, *the* shadow, *the* death, and *the* disgrace that constituted judgment on sinful Israel.[9] He will destroy for Israel the curse of warfare and destruction that also oppresses the other nations: the nations will continue to commit acts

---

8. See Wright, *Romans*, 563.

9. For the interpretation see Watts, *Isaiah 1–33*, 331–33.

of violence and brutality, but God will give peace to his people as part of the restoration of the land.[10]

For now, however, Paul is speaking for people, many of them no doubt already disenfranchised and impoverished, who must expect to face extreme hardship because they have dared to associate themselves with an anti-social Jewish reform movement that expects God to judge the world in the foreseeable future through a crucified messiah. Whatever hold death may have over humanity because of sin, he must persuade them that the gift of life exceeds it—and that they need not be afraid. The argument zigzags through a series of contrastive statements by which the "free gift" is shown to be not at all like the "trespass." In essence, whereas Adam's disobedience resulted in condemnation and death for many, Christ's obedience has resulted in something *much more*—an abundance of God's grace and life for many. But in this compressed form the argument gives us no reason for the escalation. Why should the free gift be *so much more* than the trespass? The fact that Christ was obedient whereas Adam was disobedient accounts for the contrasting outcomes—condemnation for many, justification for many—but not for the escalation. The answer appears to lie in the fact that between Adam and Christ the Law was interposed, leading to an intensification or increase of sin—and as Paul says, "where sin increased, grace abounded all the more" (5:20).[11] Given this, it is arguable that when Paul says that "the free gift following many trespasses brought justification" (5:16), he is thinking in the first place, at least, of the many trespasses of Israel that are impelling the nation towards destruction. A relevant parallel is found in 1 Esdras, where Ezra laments the mounting sins of Israel in marrying foreign wives, which led to judgment in the form of war, exile, and plunder: "For our sins have

10. If the inheritance of the "kingdom of God" in 1 Cor 15:50 refers to the moment when the suffering churches come to share in the vindication of Jesus (see Perriman, *Son of Man*, 172), it is arguable that Paul's allusion to the swallowing up of death in victory (15:54–55) carries the same covenantal restrictions: it is death *insofar as* it stands as a threat or enemy to the persecuted churches, as they live through the wrath of God, that is overcome.

11. Paul's argument in Gal 3:19 is rather different: "Why then the law? It was added because of transgressions, until the seed might come to whom it has been promised, ordained through angels by the hand of a mediator" (my translation). Here the Law is understood to have been introduced because of the transgressions of the descendants of Abraham—to keep order, so to speak, until the promise might be inherited through faith.

risen higher (*hai. . . hamartiai hēmōn epleonasan*) than our heads, and our mistakes have mounted up to heaven. . . . Because of our sins and the sins of our ancestors, we with our kindred and our kings and our priests were given over to the kings of the earth, to the sword and exile and plundering, in shame until this day" (1 Esd 8:72–74; cf. Ezra 9:6–7). It is precisely the covenant defined by the Law that gives rise both to this condemnation and to any gift of grace on the part of God that might surpass it. In any case, the expansive argument about Adam has been refocused on the question of Jewish existence: it is out of this particular narrative about judgment on Israel that grace comes to reign through righteousness to the life of the age to come.

The outcome will be life: those who have been justified by grace will not in the end be subject to death but will "reign in life" (5:17); Christ's act of righteousness has resulted in "justification of life" for all people (5:18, my translation); and grace will "reign through righteousness" leading to the life of the age that will follow judgment (5:21). The language of reigning has distinct eschatological connotations that may be relevant here: Kirk refers to the hope found in Wisdom of Solomon that the righteous "will judge Gentiles and have authority over people."[12] This thought is certainly pertinent for New Testament expectation, but the immediate significance of the language in this context derives from the contrast with the reign of death over humanity (5:17).

Baptism into the Death and Resurrection of Christ: 6:1–11

If in some sense the Law by which the world is to be held accountable has been superseded by grace (5:20–21), or if both Jews and Gentiles are now being preemptively justified *apart from works of the Law* (3:21–24), Paul has to address a question that must have been thrown at him repeatedly, perhaps sardonically, perhaps quite seriously: Should we then do evil that good things may come from it (3:8)? Should we remain in sin that grace may increase (6:1)? Are we to sin because we are not under Law but under grace (6:15)? His answer is that "we" cannot "remain in sin" because the very fact of baptism into Christ Jesus constitutes a departure from sinful Israel under condemnation. Baptism into Christ is a baptism into the narrative of his death and resurrection, which prefigures and perhaps even

---

12. Kirk, *Unlocking Romans*, 102.

encapsulates the destruction and restoration of Israel: on the one hand, the old Adamic humanity that kept Israel subject to a law of sin and death has been symbolically crucified, as Jesus was crucified by the Romans and as Israel would be crucified by the Romans; on the other, it entails a symbolic resurrection, a determination to walk now in newness of life, as Israel would be raised and restored to life (cf. Hos 6:1–2).

But there is more to this than a symbolic identification with the narrative of Jesus's death and resurrection. What Paul means by "we have become grown-together (*symphytoi*) with the likeness of his death" in 6:5 (my translation) has been much debated. The paragraph concludes with a straightforward exhortation, addressed directly to his readers in Rome, that has to do with the present self-understanding of believers: "So you also must consider yourselves dead to sin and alive to God in Christ Jesus" (6:11). But there is also an important *future* aspect to Paul's argument here: we will share in his resurrection (6:5); we will not be condemned because of sin but will be acquitted (6:7); we will live together with him, over whom death no longer has dominion (6:8). This appears to have in view something more than a symbolic participation in the resurrection of Jesus. Although Paul does not explicitly say that they will be "grown-together with the likeness of his resurrection," this is certainly required by the elliptical sentence structure in 6:5. But if this is a *real* resurrection, should we not understand the union with the likeness of his death in similar terms? Clearly he cannot mean that they have died literally, but Paul will speak in chapter 8 quite realistically of suffering together and being glorified together with Christ (8:17). If we also recall that he introduced this section by outlining an experiential process that led from justification to affliction to a confident hope in the glory of God (5:1–5), we have to take seriously the possibility that the conditional clause "*if* we have become grown-together with the likeness of his death" anticipates the "*if* indeed we suffer together . . ." of 8:17, referring therefore not to a symbolic participation in Christ's death but to the realistic experience of persecution culminating potentially in a death like his—in a Christ-like martyrdom. It seems to me that the phrase "likeness of his death/resurrection" establishes a continuity between the symbolic and the real, between the present and the future, between the potential and the eventual reality of suffering and vindication, between the baptismal event and the day when those who have made this extreme commitment may find themselves called to participate quite realistically in what Campbell correctly identifies as—though he fails to set it firmly enough within a historical framework—the "underlying martyrological narrative" of Christ's death and resurrection.[13]

It is certainly the case that Paul thought of himself and the apostles as having been called both to re-enact the sufferings of Jesus and to provide a pattern for others to follow. Because they are afflicted, perplexed, persecuted, struck down, they carry at all times in their own physical bodies the "putting to death (*nekrōsin*) of Jesus" (my translation); they are "always being given over to death for Jesus's sake" (2 Cor 4:8–11). Paul has repudiated his Jewish heritage not merely in order to gain "the righteousness from God that depends on faith" but in order to share in Christ's sufferings and become "like him in his death" in the hope of experiencing the same "resurrection from the dead" (Phil 3:8–11). He rejoices in what he is suffering for the sake of the Colossian believers because it means he is making up the shortfall between his own sufferings and Christ's for the sake of his body (Col 1:24).[14] Lopez has argued that when Paul writes in Galatians that God has revealed his Son *en emoi*, he means that "he has the dynamics of defeat by the Romans within him." He repeatedly associates himself with Jesus's crucifixion—he has been crucified with Christ, who now "lives in me (*en emoi*)" (Gal 2:20); and crucifixion, "as violent punishment of state enemies, is . . . a core image of divinely ordained Roman domination over all the nations."[15]

So we can again elucidate a basic structure of prefiguration or preemption that ties together the story of Jesus, the immediate experience of the believing communities, and the eventual justification of those communities on a day of wrath—and with that, of course, the decisive demonstration of the righteousness of Israel's God before the eyes of the nations. First, Jesus died because of the sin of Israel but was raised to newness of life. Secondly, those who are now *in Christ Jesus* have participated symbolically in his death and resurrection through baptism, which should find concrete expression in their actual lives in the present (cf. 6:11). Thirdly, this present participation in the death and resurrection to life of Jesus is a prophetic anticipation of the eventual suffering and vindication of the

13. E.g., Campbell, *Deliverance of God*, 647–56.

14. For the exegesis see Perriman, *Son of Man*, 103–4.

15. Lopez, *Apostle*, 135.

churches at a time of wrath, during the birth pains of the (historically conceived) age to come. Paul argues in these chapters for the participation of the believer in the Christ event, but it is not the Christ event that is "era-shifting," as Kirk has it.[16] The "era-shifting" moment is still to come, but it has been anticipated in the existence of a faithful community that has participated in the Christ event and replicates in its shared life the righteousness that will eventually force the issue eschatologically.

The Benchmark of Righteousness: 6:12—7:6

This righteousness cannot be merely notional, not merely forensic: the faithfulness of the community will be expressed not least in its resolute adherence to a standard of righteousness that will be determinative for the transformation that lies ahead. So Paul is thankful that the saints in Rome have not only been set free from sin but have become "obedient from the heart to the standard of teaching to which you were committed" (6:17). When they were slaves of sin, the fruit was "things of which you are now ashamed," the end of which—the wages for which—would be the death that is prescribed by the Law for habitually sinful Israel (6:20–21, 23). Now, however, they have presented the members of their bodies to God as "weapons (*hopla*) of righteousness" (6:13), they have become "slaves of righteousness," and will have "your fruit for consecration (*hagiasmon*) and the outcome life of the age," which is the "free gift" or *charisma* of God (6:22, my translation). I suggest that this still directly and substantively presupposes the eschatological narrative of suffering and vindication that frames Romans 5–8. The fruitfulness of righteous Israel is a prominent eschatological motif (Isa 32:15–17; 60:21; Hos 10:12; Amos 6:12; *Jub.* 1.16). The "free gift of God" is the act of obedience after Israel's "many trespasses" that ensures that many will find the life of the age to come (5:15–21). Paul will inform the saints in Rome in chapter 13 that the night is far advanced, the day is at hand; they should "cast off the works of darkness and put on the armor (*hopla*) of light" (13:12), because a conflict is approaching. This is the circumstance for which they are consecrated. Actual works of righteousness, equivalent to the righteousness demanded by the Law, will be instrumental in enabling the churches to make the transition to the age that will follow the public vindication of

16. Kirk, *Unlocking Romans*, 98.

Jesus and of those who have faithfully identified themselves with his dying and resurrection.

Israel under the Law remained trapped in destructive patterns of behavior and could only "bear fruit for death." Israel "released from the Law" by its close identification with Jesus, who was repudiated by the rulers of Jerusalem, who became accursed according to the Law, who anticipated in his own body the destruction that would come upon the people as a whole, is in a position to "bear fruit for God," to "serve in the new way of the Spirit and not in the old way of the written code" (7:4–6). The contextual force of the argument is recovered when we set it against the backdrop of a passage such as *4 Ezra* 3.20–27, which offers, under the guise of a lament on the Babylonian invasion, a post-AD 70 Jewish reflection on the failure of the Law to prevent the war and the destruction of Jerusalem: "Yet you did not take away from them their evil heart, so that your Law might bring forth fruit in them. For the first Adam, burdened with an evil heart, transgressed and was overcome, as were all who were descended from him. Thus the disease became permanent; the law was in the people's heart along with the evil root, but what was good departed, and the evil remained." David built a city for YHWH, where oblations were offered for many years; "but the inhabitants of the city transgressed, in everything doing as Adam and all his descendants had done, for they also had the evil heart. So you delivered the city into the hands of your enemies" (cf. *4 Ezra* 4.23; 9.37). This is exactly Paul's argument in Romans, except that in *4 Ezra*, with the benefit of hindsight, the political outcome has become unambiguous: because Israel failed to keep the Law, Jerusalem was given into the hands of its enemies.

As things turned out, the righteousness of the Christians would indeed account substantially for their eventual victory over paganism. David Bentley Hart observes, "the distinctive behavior of Christians—including temperance, gentleness, lawfulness, and acts of supererogatory kindness—not only was visible to their neighbors outside the faith but constituted a large part of the new faith's appeal." He cites the begrudging acknowledgment of the emperor Julian: "It is [the Christians'] philanthropy towards strangers, the care they take of the graves of the dead, and the affected sanctity with which they conduct their lives that have done most to spread their atheism."[17] We see here, in thoroughly realistic

17. Hart, *Atheist Delusions*, 153–54.

terms, what it would mean for these consecrated "saints," set free from their slavery to sin, to provide the benchmark of righteousness by which God would expose the moral and spiritual bankruptcy of the old world.

10

The Very Difficult Path Leading to Life

Paul's argument about judgment and righteousness presupposes the prophetic conviction, which goes back to John the Baptist and Jesus, that national Israel is complacently travelling a broad road leading to political-religious disaster. The alternative is a narrow and difficult path leading to life; and it is made clear enough that if the disciples of Jesus wish to follow him down that path, they will have to endure their own version of the cross—not as a matter of pious metaphor but as a distressing reality, the theological significance of which modern Western interpreters, still securely ensconced in a protective tradition of religious tolerance (or indifference), find hard to register. The way of salvation for this nascent community of renewed Israel would inevitably be a way of suffering. Paul, too, is fully persuaded that those who have been justified and have found peace with God boast not only in their hope of the glory of God but also in their sufferings (Rom 5:1–5). Experience has already taught him this (e.g., 1 Cor 4:8–13; 2 Cor 11:23–27); but as he sets out the implications of his gospel for the believers in Rome, we may also imagine that, like the Jewish war, Nero's persecution of the "saints" casts its grim backward shadow over his mind. Romans 8 is written under that shadow.

The Spirit of Christ: 8:1–17

So, Paul roundly declares, there can be no condemnation for those in Christ Jesus. The logic of sin and death, by which the Law that determined blessing and chastisement for Israel was disastrously circumscribed, which now fundamentally called into question the whole extravagant notion that a people could live in authentic relationship with God and be a blessing to the nations rather than an embarrassment, has been broken. There *will be* no condemnation of those who have been preemptively justified by their trust in the precedent of Jesus, who exercise the same practical faithfulness, when their world is engulfed in the destruction and persecution and turmoil and terrorization of the day of wrath. What the Law was unable to achieve *for Israel* because Israel's "flesh" was so weak, God achieved *for his people* by sending his own Son "in the likeness of sinful flesh and for sin," so that the "righteous requirement of the law might be fulfilled in us, who walk not according to the flesh but according to the Spirit" (8:3–4). This is a crucial statement and needs to be carefully disassembled if we are to understand how it works.

The first thing to note is that this is not an argument about the salvation of humanity. The Law was never intended to *save* or *justify* humanity. It was one of the advantages that Israel possessed (cf. Rom 3:1–2); and it failed to preserve Israel because it was "weakened by the flesh"—it could not correct Israel's essential human sinfulness. So what God achieved by sending his own Son was *for the sake of that people* that stood condemned by the Law and faced destruction within a generation of Jesus's death. It is the same restriction that we find in the words of the angel to Joseph: "you shall call his name Jesus, for he will save *his people* from their sins" (Matt 1:21).

Secondly, it is only of incidental interest here—but of interest nevertheless—that the famous Priene Calendar Inscription (c. 9 BC) tells of the decision made by the "Greeks of Asia" to honor the birthday of Augustus, whom Providence had *sent* (*pempsasa*) "as a savior (*sōtēra*), both for us and for our descendants, that he might end war and arrange all things"— his birthday being the "beginning of the good tidings (*euangeliōn*) for the world that came by reason of him."[1] Augustus, of course, is *divi filius*, *theou huios*, and on the whole it seems unlikely that in this context Paul's language of God having sent (*pempsas*) his own Son carries any stronger incarnational overtones than are suggested by the analogy with imperial rhetoric. But that is merely to highlight the fact that the christological

---

1. For the translation see Evans, "Mark's Incipit," 68–69. "(Divine) providence" (*pronoia*) is a common signifier for God in Hellenistic Jewish writings (e.g., 4 Macc 17:22; Wis 17:2).

categories of Christendom need to be thoroughly re-examined—not necessarily downgraded—in the light of the eschatological narratives that control Paul's thought.

Thirdly, in his introductory statement about the "gospel of God," Paul wrote that it had to do with "his Son, who was descended from David according to the flesh" (Rom 1:3). If he now speaks of Jesus having been sent "in likeness of a flesh of sin" (my translation), I would suggest that this "flesh" is Israel's rather than Adam's: behind the compressed phrasing lies a story of Jesus's *apparent* implication in Israel's rebelliousness—his death, in the end, *looked like* God's judgment on Israel by the agency of Rome. The argument may be broken down into the following parts: 1) the "flesh" here is what bound Jesus as God's Son, descended from David, to his people; 2) Israel's "flesh" has proved to be incorrigibly sinful, hostile in mind to God, unable to submit to the Law of God or to please God (Rom 8:7–8); and 3) Jesus, though not rebellious himself but obedient to his prophetic (cf. Jer 1:7–8) or messianic sending, became so embroiled in Israel's story that it looked to all the world as though he himself were sinful. He *looked like* just another reckless, renegade Jew executed for a half-hearted and ill-conceived attempt to mount an insurgency against Rome. We find just this argument in Wisdom of Solomon. The righteous are unjustly put to death by corrupt rulers, resentful of their reproaches and their pretension to be counted as divine sons; they appeared in the sight of men to have been punished for a crime but were nevertheless accepted by God as a "sacrificial whole burnt offering" (Wis 3:4–6). Jesus is likewise the righteous one, who *appeared* to have been punished as a presumptuous and disloyal Jew, but whose sacrifice has been accepted by God.

Fourthly, this death as part of Israel's story and at the hand of Israel's enemies was not at all a mistake but was "for sin" (*peri hamartias*)—a phrase that is used widely in the Septuagint to denote a "sin offering" brought before the Lord. As in the old stories of the Maccabean martyrs, the death of an innocent righteous man came to be interpreted as a sacrifice that would atone for the sins of the people and deliver them from the wrath of God. Narratively speaking, Jesus's death differed from these prototypes only inasmuch as he was physically raised by God on the third day—as a sign to those who saw and believed that Israel's hopes of being healed and restored following judgment were coming to fulfillment in him (cf. Hos 6:1–2).

Finally, the outcome, as Paul states it here, is that the "righteous requirement (*dikaiōma*) of the law might be fulfilled" in a people that is not captive to the flesh, as Israel was, but lives according to the Spirit. The point is not simply that Christians should be righteous as a matter of principle: there is a specific purpose entailed. It is a fundamental premise of Paul's gospel that God will hold the *oikoumenē* accountable in the foreseeable future. Israel, as a people in possession of the Law, ought to have provided the benchmark of righteousness by which God would judge the world. It has not done so—indeed, it has failed to the extent that it faces destruction. It falls, therefore, to those who walk not according to the flesh but according to the Spirit to embody the standard by which the pagan world will be held accountable. Significantly, *dikaiōma* is used earlier in Romans to denote a standard of righteousness that could properly be demanded from Gentiles (1:32; 2:26).

At this point the argument takes the critical turn that was hinted at in 6:5–11. The Spirit of God that gives life to those who have been preemptively justified, by which they are enabled to fulfill the "righteous requirement of the Law," is the Spirit of Christ; it is a Spirit that intimately connects them with the story of Jesus. Those who have the Spirit of Christ "belong to him"; Christ is in them; and the God who "raised Christ Jesus from the dead will also give life to your mortal bodies through his Spirit who dwells in you" (8:9–11). This is not the symbolic language of death and life, represented in the event of baptism and worked out in the present as a departure from Israel according to sinful flesh and a new life of righteousness. It is certainly not the inflated and largely superfluous language of Christian conversion. Paul is beginning to speak here of a realistic participation in the story of Jesus's suffering and resurrection: to have the Spirit of Jesus is to have the assurance that God will raise their mortal, martyred bodies from the dead, just as he raised Jesus from the dead. What stands in the way of this is the flesh, because the flesh is rebellious, disobedient, sinful, unable to please God; the flesh will cause them to fall back into fear when affliction comes (8:15); in the language of Hebrews 10:38, echoing Habakkuk 2:3–4, it will make them "shrink back." But if, symbolically, by the power of the Spirit of Jesus, they put to death the deeds of the body, if they crucify the flesh with its passions and desires, if they die to the world, as Paul himself has done (Gal 5:24; 6:14), they become "sons of God"—Jesus-like in a very specific sense. Paul is describing a martyr spirituality.

In the first place, this is a Spirit by which those who have been adopted as sons cry "Abba, Father" (8:15). This appeal, of course, was found on the lips of Jesus in Gethsemane as he considered the suffering that he would soon have to endure: "Remove this cup from me; but not what I wish, but what you wish" (Mark 14:36). Commentators tend to regard the utterance as at most a general recollection of Jesus's manner of prayer,[2] but for Paul to invoke this distressed appeal to God and its painful narrative context at this juncture can hardly be accidental. He expects the "saints" to have to make the same appeal when the cup of God's wrath comes round to them (cf. Ps 75:8; Isa 51:17, 22; Jer 49:12; Lam 2:13 LXX; 4:21; Ezek 23:31–34; Hab 2:16).

If they are "sons," they are by definition also heirs: "heirs of God," in the first place, which echoes Old Testament language of a special relationship between God and his people and, no doubt, the specific expectation that the descendants of Abraham would inherit the world (cf. Rom 4:19); but also *potentially* "fellow heirs with Christ, *provided* we suffer with him in order that we may also be glorified with him" (8:17). Here Paul states very clearly what it means to be "fellow heirs (*synklēronomoi*) with Christ." It is a status strictly and expressly contingent upon (*eiper*) participation in the narrative of Christ's suffering and glorification. To be an heir *with Christ* of any future inheritance is not to shrink back in fear of the day of wrath but to "cry out" to God who is "father"—*krazō* is often used in the Septuagint, notably in the Psalms, for the cry of the afflicted to God for deliverance from their suffering (e.g., Exod 22:22; Jdg 3:9, 15; 4:3; 18:24; Pss 3:5; 4:4; 18:6; 22:2, 24; 31:22; 34:6; 107:6; Hab 1:2; 1 Macc 9:46). To be an heir with Christ is to emulate the extreme trust in the face of suffering that Jesus demonstrated in Gethsemane.[3] To be an heir with Christ, in other words, is to walk a narrow and difficult pathway leading to persecution and, potentially at least, martyrdom. What Paul has in view here is the same specific prospect of imitating Jesus in his death and resurrection

---

2. E.g., Dunn, *Romans 1–8*, 453–54; Wright, *Romans*, 593: "It was a way, above all, of making Jesus' prayers one's own, and hence of sharing the sonship of Jesus."

3. The contextual significance is not so apparent in Gal 4:5–6, though 5:5 suggests an eschatological framework for understanding the experience of the Spirit.

that he appropriates for himself in a more personal manner in Philippians 3:10–14.[4]

The Sufferings of the Present Time: 8:18–38

The thoroughgoing eschatological character of the argument is brought out in the second half of Romans 8. In the first place, the sufferings of the *present* time are contrasted with the glory that is *about to be* (*mellousan*) revealed in the "sons of God" at the redemption of their bodies (8:18). The phrase "sons of God" would normally be understood as a reference to the elected status of Israel among the nations (Rom 8:19; cf. Deut 14:1; Hos 1:10; 3 Macc 6:28; *Pss. Sol.* 17.27). Paul will quote Hosea 1:10 in this sense in Romans 9:26; and in Galatians 3:26 "sons of God" denotes a radically reconstituted people of God in Christ. In the immediate context, however, which speaks of the "sons of God" as having put to death the deeds of the body, suffering, and awaiting vindication, the influence of Jewish martyr traditions, albeit reinterpreted, cannot be discounted. Wisdom of Solomon, for example, describes how the righteous will stand vindicated in the presence of the wicked who scorned and afflicted them, who will ask, "How are they counted among sons of God, and how is their inheritance among saints?" (Wis 5:5, my translation; cf. 2:18). Paul's language may even hint at the same surprise on the part of unrighteous Israel when it becomes apparent that this Jewish break-away movement was justified in putting its faith in Jesus.

Just as creation waits for deliverance from its bondage to decay and death, those who suffer as Christ suffered wait "with endurance" (*di' hypomonēs*). "Endurance" is a cardinal eschatological virtue. We have already heard Paul argue that their afflictions produce endurance (*hypomonēn*) and endurance produces a tested character, which gives grounds for their hope that when the day of wrath irrupts into the midst of history, they will be saved by Jesus's life (Rom 5:3–10). A passage from Luke's Gospel shows how the statement might be situated in a realistic eschatological self-awareness. Jesus speaks of the hostility that his followers will face in the period preceding the desolation of Jerusalem by the armies of Titus, when there will be "great distress upon the land and wrath against this people" (Luke 21:23, my translation). They will be tried

---

4. See Perriman, *Son of Man*, 104–5.

in the synagogues and imprisoned; they will be brought before kings and governors because of their witness to Jesus; they will be delivered up by family and friends; and they will be hated by all. But not a hair of your head will perish: "by your endurance (*hypomenē*) you gained your souls" (Luke 21:18–19, my translation; also 4 Macc 1:11; 9:30; 17:23; Rom 15:4; 2 Cor 1:6; 6:4; 2 Thess 1:4). This is not far at all from Habakkuk's assurance that when the Chaldeans descend upon Israel, the righteous person will live by his faith.

The Spirit by which Jesus cried out, "Abba, Father," as he confronted the fear of death, will be with the saints in their weakness, interceding "with groanings too deep for words" (8:26–27). They are confident that everything works together for good for those who love God and who are "called according to his purpose," because it is precisely God's intention that others would emulate Jesus's suffering and glorification: others would be "conformed to the image of his Son"; he would be "firstborn among many brothers" (8:28–29).[5] Again we have a realistic, non-mythical, and directly pertinent pattern of eschatological replication. Jesus's dying and coming to life are partly reproduced in the present experience of those who have been baptized into him, in the experience of the Spirit that comforts and fortifies. But they will be replicated fully under extreme future conditions when those who have been predestined, called, and justified will suffer and be glorified. It should be clear enough that "predestination" does not here signify a general Christian privilege: it is a name for the exceptional calling that is placed on those who would suffer as Christ suffered.

So Witherington and Hyatt correctly note that Paul shares the Jewish notion of a limited "resurrection of the righteous or saints," of which Jesus was the firstfruits.[6] But what Paul describes in Romans 8:18–39 is such a specific, imitative participation of the saints in the story of Jesus's death and resurrection that we must conclude that he is much more consistent

---

5. The idea of being conformed to the "image" of Jesus is also found in 2 Cor 3:18: "we all, with unveiled face, beholding the glory of the Lord, are being transformed into the same image from one degree of glory to another." Although we instinctively want to read this as a general account of Christian transformation, it is integral to an argument in which the suffering and glorification of Jesus is replicated, primarily, in the experience of Paul and his companions, and secondarily, and less certainly, in the experience of the Corinthians.

6. Witherington and Hyatt, *Romans*, 33.

in his use of the Jewish template than Witherington and Hyatt in practice allow. The observation cannot be reconciled with conventional eschatological schemata that treat Jesus's resurrection simply as the anomalous antecedent for a general resurrection of all the dead. Rather, Paul is working with an underlying narrative according to which it is the suffering of the communities of the saints, the "sons of God," across the *oikoumenē* that would inaugurate the eschaton and bring about the reign of God over the whole world. But this transformative event was anticipated in the death and resurrection of Jesus, who was the "firstborn among many brothers" (8:29), the "firstfruits" of those who would die and be made alive "in Christ" (1 Cor 15:20–23), the "firstborn from the dead" (Col 1:18). In the language of Revelation, when the suffering church is finally vindicated against its savage pagan opponent, those who were killed "for the testimony of Jesus and for the word of God," who did not worship the beast or its image, will come to life in a "first resurrection" and reign with Christ for a thousand years—that is, until a second resurrection and a final judgment of *all the dead* (Rev 20:4–6, 11–15).

The misfortunes listed in 8:35 are not the routine afflictions of humankind; they are those that Paul endured for the sake of Christ: danger, hunger, nakedness, distress, and persecutions (cf. 2 Cor 11:23–27; 12:10).[7] Remarkably, they are the sufferings that Jesus warned his "brothers" would face as they confronted—indeed *affronted*—both Judaism and the *oikoumenē* with the announcement that God was about to act as king to deliver his faithful people and punish his enemies: hunger, thirst, nakedness, sickness, imprisonment, and the neglect and contempt of the unrighteous (Matt 25:31–36). The assurance is that none of this would separate them from the "love of Christ." Just as the Maccabean martyrs "conquered (*nikēsantes*) the tyrant by their endurance" Antiochus Epiphanes (4 Macc 1:11), so the "elect of God" will "conquer completely (*hypernikōmen*) through the one who loved us" (8:37). The quotation of Psalm 44:22, finally, in Romans 8:36 makes it clear that the "sufferings of the present time," which will culminate in glory, presuppose a context of eschatological conflict. Israel has been routed in battle and scattered; they have become "a byword among the nations, a laughingstock among the

---

7. Against Moo, *Romans*, 511: "These 'sufferings of the present time' are not only those 'trials' that are endured directly because of the confession of Christ—for instance, persecution—but encompass the whole gamut of suffering, including such things as illness, bereavement, hunger, financial reverses, and death itself."

peoples" (44:14). Suffering has come upon them even though they have been faithful to YHWH: "All this has come upon us, though we have not forgotten you, and we have not been false to your covenant. . . . Yet for your sake we are killed all the day long; we are regarded as sheep to be slaughtered" (44:17, 22). The suffering of righteous Israel and the urgent expression of hope that YHWH will deliver them "for the sake of your steadfast love" are a template for Paul's reassurance to the saints in Rome that no powers in creation—not even the power of Caesar himself, though this is not Paul's particular argument—can separate them "from the love of God in Christ Jesus our Lord" (Rom 8:39).

The martyrological intent of Paul's language and its profound significance for the future of the people of God can also be roughly indicated by looking ahead to accounts of Christian martyrdom. Ignatius of Antioch spoke of death from wild beasts in the arena as a way of gaining Jesus Christ (Ign. *Rom.* 5). Polycarp exhorts the Philippians to practice the obedience and "endurance" (*hypomonēn*) that they have seen exemplified both in their contemporaries, including Ignatius, and in Paul and the apostles. Just as Paul informs the Thessalonians that the dead will not be excluded from the vindication of the people of God (1 Thess 4:13–18),[8] he assures them that the martyrs have not run in vain but are now "with the Lord in the 'place which is their due,' with whom they also suffered" (Pol. *Phil.* 9, LCL). The martyrs are "imitators (*mimētas*) of the Lord" (*Mart. Pol.* 17.3). The account of the persecutions in Gaul under Marcus Aurelius, cited at length by Eusebius, describes the heroic faith of believers who "endured every punishment as they hurried to Christ, proving that the sufferings of this present time are not worthy to be compared with the glory that shall be revealed in us" (Eusebius *Hist. eccl.* 5.1.6); he says that they were "so eager to imitate Christ" that they refused to accept the name of "martyr," which should belong to Christ alone, the "true Martyr and Firstborn from the dead" (5.2.3). Dionysius wrote concerning those who died under Decius that they are now "seated with Christ, and are sharers in his kingdom, partakers of his judgment and judges with him" (6.42.5).

It is apparent that this language presupposes a more or less coherent eschatological narrative and that this narrative overlaps substantially with Paul's argument concerning a community that would have to suffer with

8. See Perriman, *Son of Man*, 174–75.

Christ in order to be glorified with Christ: those who patiently endure affliction and are killed are imitators of Christ (cf. 1 Thess 1:6; 2 Thess 2:14; cf. Heb 6:11), they attain Christ (cf. Phil 3:8–11), they are raised after him who is the firstborn (cf. Rom 8:29; 1 Cor 15:20; 1 Thess 4:16), have entered into his presence, are seated with him at the right hand of God, and reign with him (cf. 1 Thess 4:17; Rev 20:6).[9] We should not underestimate the historical significance of this narrative. Brown makes the point that in the ancient world "the Christian idea of martyrdom was a dangerous novelty" that turned the religious life of the cities into a battlefield—it represented a "fully public clash of gods." The fact is that in concrete terms the victory of Christ over the gods of the nations was realized just through this Jesus-like suffering, this obstinate, self-sacrificing defiance of the "rulers and authorities" in the knowledge that their power to destroy had been disabled by the cross (Col 2:15)—"O death, where is your victory? O death, where is your sting?" (1 Cor 15:55). This is what it meant to have the Spirit of Jesus, to be conformed to his image. Accounts of the martyrs never emphasized their human courage. "Rather," Brown says, "the martyrs were presented as men and women possessed by the power of Christ. They had a mighty God in them, and, by their heroic deaths, they trumped the power of the ancient gods of the city."[10]

The Eager Longing of Creation: 8:19–23

We have until now skirted round what Paul has to say about creation in this passage (8:19–23). If we are to situate his gospel and the arguments that he develops around it in a proximate historical narrative, what are we to make of the apparent association of the liberation of the sons of God with the liberation of the whole of creation? If the wrath and salvation that Paul envisages were to be realized in such events as the Jewish War, the sporadic but intense persecution of the churches, the eventual collapse of Greco-Roman paganism, and the legitimization of Christianity by Constantine . . . well, the problem is obvious: this historical transformation, massively significant as it was, did not include the final transformation of the cosmos.

9. For the argument generally see Perriman, *Son of Man*.

10. Brown, *Western Christendom*, 66.

The expectation that creation will be liberated from its bondage to decay cannot be less realistic than the expectation that the sons of God will overcome death. The background to the thought is found in Isaiah's vision of the land of Israel corrupted by the sin of its inhabitants: "The land shall be corrupted with corruption (*phthorai phtharēsetai*), and the land shall be spoiled with spoiling" (Isa 24:3 LXX, my translation). The restoration of Israel following exile, therefore, may be described *poetically* as a renewal of creation: "For the Lord comforts Zion; he comforts all her waste places and makes her wilderness like Eden, her desert like the garden of the Lord . . ." (Isa 51:3). But the resurrection of Jesus *from the dead* has introduced an ontological novelty—it is the beginning of a literal *new* creation—and has given rise to the hope not merely that others might be raised in similar fashion but that the whole cosmos might be transformed.

The question, then, is whether in 8:19–23 Paul understands the liberation of the sons of God from their sufferings and the liberation of the whole of creation from its slavery to decay to be part of the same final, cosmic event. If he does, then we must either revert to the conventional schema, which pushes the apocalyptic outcome into the remote future and rather makes a mockery of the pervasive sense of urgent expectation that is as apparent in Romans as anywhere else in the New Testament; or we must assume that Paul was mistaken in thinking that the coming judgment would trigger a cataclysm of cosmic proportions. A modern analogy, however, may point towards a reading of Paul's argument in this passage that permits us to preserve *both* the historical contingency of the apocalyptic argument *and* the finality of the hope in a new creation.

Over the 28 years that the "Anti-Fascist Protection Wall" divided East and West Germany there were about 5,000 successful (and perhaps a couple of hundred unsuccessful) escape attempts from East to West. Let us imagine that the people of East Germany, having been subjected to futility, so to speak, groaned together as though in childbirth, longing for the day when the wall would be torn down and they would be liberated as a nation. They would surely have seen in the isolated dramas of defection, in the risky escape of a select few from captivity to freedom, a *prefiguring* of their own eventual liberation and a reason to hope that the existing state of affairs would not last forever.

I would suggest that Paul is telling a similar two-stage story about liberation. First, at a time of wrath, those who trust in Jesus, who have been justified by that trust, will be saved by his life (5:9–10). They participate quite literally in the eschatological drama anticipated in Jesus's suffering and resurrection, and in the end they are vindicated. They are the reckless defectors, the select few, who escape prematurely from death to life. The point is variously made: a glory is revealed in them; the sons of God are revealed to the world; they are adopted as sons; their bodies are redeemed from suffering and death (8:18–23). In retrospect at least, it appears that there are two sides to this moment of historical vindication. For those who in this way are indeed conformed to the image of the Son of God, it is a final victory over death, a resurrection to the right hand of the Father to reign with Christ throughout the coming ages. For the persecuted churches of the *oikoumenē*, however, it is the ending of their affliction and the public vindication of a monotheistic movement that defied both Judaism and paganism in its radical loyalty to the God who promised Abraham that his offspring would inherit the world. In effect, this is the distinction that is made in 1 Thessalonians 4:15–17 between those who are raised from the dead at the *parousia* event and the living community that is delivered from suffering and caught up in clouds with them to participate in the vindication of the Son of Man.[11]

In Paul's imagination, however, a personified creation, deeply implicated in the consequences of human sin, clutches eagerly at this *parousia* hope. Creation itself, which has been subjected to futility, is said to await not its own redemption but the vindication of the suffering church in the foreseeable future—the deliverance from persecution, the victory over paganism and superstition—because it knows that it will also share finally, in an *unforeseeable* future, in the glory and the freedom from corruption that will be revealed in the sons of God, in the fellow heirs of Christ, in the brothers of Jesus, in the oppressed community of the Son of Man. The redemption of these martyrs' physical, created bodies must entail the final redemption of the whole of God's creation.

11. Perriman, *Son of Man*, 164–65.

The Future of the People of God

We cannot read Romans 8, therefore, simply as a classic statement of personal salvation and the hope of eternal life. There is some point to describing it as the "inner sanctuary within the cathedral of Christian faith; the tree of life in the midst of the Garden of Eden; the highest peak in a range of mountains," but not because it constitutes a "rich and comprehensive portrayal of what it means to be a Christian"—certainly not in the modern sense in which Douglas Moo intends that designation.[12] It sits at the center of an argument about momentous social-religious transformation in the ancient world. It describes the condition of a primarily Jewish community, joined by growing numbers of enthusiastic Gentile proselytes, that has self-consciously distanced itself from Torah-based Judaism and has begun to present itself as a community of the eschatological Spirit—that is, a community that over time will embody in its life and practices, in its living and dying, prophetically and actually, the world-changing presence of Israel's God. The pattern for this experience is the living and dying of Jesus—the firstborn of many martyrs, the originator and perfecter of the faithfulness of those who must "run with endurance the race that is set before us" (Heb 12:1–2). The chapter sets out the profound but contingent hope that this community has, as it faces the afflictions that will be so graphically described in the martyrologies of the early church, of participating not only in the sufferings of Jesus but also in his resurrection and in the vindication that Paul is quite certain will come when God judges the *oikoumenē*, both the Jew first, and the Greek.

Does this mean that the chapter has no relevance for the "post-eschatological" church? No, for two reasons. First, we remain the product and beneficiaries of this eschatological narrative. The church became what it has been in the world for the last 1700 years only because of the extreme and barely comprehensible faithfulness of those who were willing to be conformed to the image of the Son "who died—more than that, who was raised—who is at the right hand of God, who indeed is interceding" (8:34) for the suffering saints of the Most High. There would have been no victory over paganism, no vindication, no future, if real communities of real people had not been willing to take up their cross and lose their lives for Jesus's sake and for the gospel.

12. Moo, *Romans*, 467–68.

Secondly, like the whole of creation, we may look to the reality of the historical transformation that took place, anticipated in the resurrection of Jesus from the dead, and find in it grounds for believing that all things will be made new. Within the New Testament resurrection belongs, for the most part, to a circumscribed Jewish story about how the righteous among a people under judgment are vindicated and rewarded—and how through their faith(fulness) the historical community is restored to wholeness and life. But the resurrection of Jesus was not a mere metaphor. It was an ontological novelty that could not be accommodated—or at least, only ambiguously and for not more than forty days—in a creation subject to decay. There must, therefore, in principle, be a new creation, a new heaven and a new earth, in which God "will wipe away every tear from their eyes, and death shall be no more, neither shall there be mourning, nor crying, nor pain anymore, for the former things have passed away" (Rev 21:4); and we trust the conviction of the far-sighted John that this final re-creation will be preceded by a resurrection of all the dead and a final judgment "according to what they had done" (Rev 20:12–13).

11

The Salvation of All Israel and Why It Didn't Happen

The anguished lament with which Paul resumes the argument about Israel in Romans 9 reveals just how profoundly personal this crisis of judgment and renewal was for him. There is certainly a seam in the text to be explained and a substantial change of topic. If the main part of the letter is a rehearsal of Paul's gospel, developed as an argument about the historical vindication of Israel's God and the perturbing implications this has for a justified community, the disjuncture already appears much less pronounced than has often been supposed. Romans 5–8 is no less narratively and historically conditioned than the opening argument about the impending wrath of God or the ensuing discussion of Israel's fate in chapters 9–11. We can point, however, to a tighter stitching between these sections. In chapter 8 Paul has presented with considerable passion the participation of the suffering church in the story of Jesus. It is the means by which these "sons of God" will be conformed to the image of Christ in glory, becoming *brothers* of Jesus, who was firstborn from the dead. But this intensely felt association with Christ only serves to exacerbate his sense of alienation from the Israelites, who are "my *brothers*, my kinsmen according to the flesh." It is around this dilemma, cutting to the heart of Paul's own religious allegiance, that the argument is hinged. The people that now finds itself devoted to destruction—*anathema*, cut off from Christ, as Paul could almost wish himself to be—nevertheless possessed the adoption, the glory, the covenants, the giving of the Law, the worship, the promises, the patriarchs, and the Messiah. How can a narrative of such immense significance suddenly come to nothing? Has the word of God failed?

Has the Word of God Failed? 9:6-33

The answer that Paul gives is "no," for the reason that "not all who are from Israel are Israel"; not all who are physically descended from Abraham have the status of "children" (9:6-7, my translation; cf. 2:28-29). For as Paul argued in chapter 4, what originally guaranteed a posterity for Abraham was neither biological descent nor adherence to the Law of Moses but the promise of God. In the same way, he makes the point that Jacob was chosen before the two children existed to do either good or evil. Rebecca was told before the birth that the "older will serve the younger" (9:10-13; cf. Gen 25:23). Israel is chosen as a matter of divine preference, not of merit: "Jacob I loved, but Esau I hated" (cf. Mal 1:2-3).

In his imagination Paul is now back in the synagogue, under interrogation; and the rhetoric of debate and polemic is rekindled. "Is there injustice on God's part?" But a Jew can hardly complain of the arbitrary nature of God's actions. Did not God say to Moses, "I will have mercy on whom I have mercy, and I will have compassion on whom I have compassion" (cf. Exod 33:19)? Did he not harden Pharaoh's heart in order to show his power and that his name might be proclaimed in all the earth (cf. Exod 9:16)? Clearly, then, "he has mercy on whomever he wills, and he hardens whomever he wills" (Rom 9:18).

But if that is the case, "Why does he still find fault? For who can resist his will?" Again, it is the fundamental credibility and integrity and righteousness of their common God that is in dispute. Paul's argument with the synagogues is that it is precisely in order to be vindicated—that is, shown to be righteous, powerful, credible—that God now has mercy on some and hardens the hearts of others. The impending crisis of judgment against both Jew and Greek and of salvation for both Jew and Greek is the means by which, in the foreseeable future, God will show his power and by which his name will be proclaimed throughout the *oikoumenē*. As in the case of the exodus and the humiliation of Pharaoh, widespread public recognition that YHWH is God and that the gods of the nations are impotent will be gained through the narrative of judgment and deliverance.

When Paul accuses his interlocutor of answering back to God in the manner of a clay pot inexcusably quarrelling with its potter—"Why have you made me like this?"—the figure immediately casts the Jew in the role of recalcitrant Israel. The vessel that presumes to question its maker is also the vessel that is destined for destruction. The image was commonplace. Hellenistic Judaism was likely to turn it against the Gentiles: the potter fashions worthless clay idols because he does not know the God who molded him (Wis 15:7–13); all humans are like a potter's clay in the hands of God "to fashion it according to his liking . . . , to repay them according to his judgment" (Sir 33:13); the lawless nations are to be driven from Jerusalem, their arrogance smashed "like a potter's vessel," their substance shattered "with an iron rod" (*Pss. Sol.* 17.22–25; cf. Ps 2:9). But for Paul it is the Old Testament antecedents that are determinative. Isaiah warns that a people who honors God with their lips but whose hearts are far from him should not imagine that God does not see their deeds and their thoughts: the clay pot cannot say of its maker, "He did not make me. . . . He has no understanding" (Isa 29:13–16). Jeremiah watches the potter break the ill-formed clay in his hands and remake it into another vessel, "as it seemed good to the potter to do"; and he hears the Lord speak to him: "O house of Israel, can I not do with you as this potter has done? declares the Lord. Behold, like the clay in the potter's hand, so are you in my hand, O house of Israel" (Jer 18:1–6). If God is intent on "shaping disaster" against unrighteous Israel (18:11), they have no grounds for complaint.

This is the situation that the Jews now face. Although God has desired to show his anger towards rebellious Israel and make known his power in the ancient world,[1] he has "endured with much patience" clay pots that have been prepared for destruction—not an abstract or final judgment, but a contextualized, historical, calamitous judgment on a "crooked generation" (cf. Acts 2:40). The other side of the coin is that God has, in the meantime, in this breathing space, made known the "riches of his glory for vessels of mercy" (Rom 9:23): the mixed communities of Jews and Gentiles exist as a concrete and visible demonstration to the world that the God who brings an end to derelict and delinquent systems of belief and practice, whether Jewish or pagan, also creates something new. This

---

1. This takes the participle *thelōn* as concessive rather than causal (cf. Wright, *Romans*, 641).

is a restatement of the argument of Romans 3:25–26: in this present time when God has overlooked the former sins of Israel and judgment has been postponed, he has shown himself to be righteous by putting forward Jesus as an atonement so that those who are justified by their faith or trust may live when eventually the day of wrath comes.

The argument is backed up, finally, with quotations from Hosea and Isaiah. Two points are made. First, Hosea speaks of the restoration of a people whom YHWH has disowned because of their idolatry: they will be called "my people," "beloved," and "sons of the living God" (9:25–26; cf. Hos 1:10; 2:23). Paul appears to take "not my people," however, to include Gentiles. Secondly, we have statements from Isaiah that restrict those who are saved—who survive the catastrophe of judgment—to a remnant. Otherwise, there would be no "seed" left, no descendants for Abraham, no fulfillment of the promise: they would be wiped off the face of the earth like the residents of Sodom and Gomorrah (Isa 1:9; 10:22–23). This is the point of the question that is put to Jesus: "Lord, will those who are saved be few?" (Luke 13:23). Jesus's answer—that they should struggle (*agōnizesthe*) to enter by a narrow door because many will be excluded from this difficult salvation—stands as a defining motif for Paul's extended argument with the Jews.

The right of God both to judge and to reconstitute Israel has been established; now we go back to the fundamental matter at hand. The nations did not pursue righteousness, but they have been justified by virtue of their unexpected willingness to believe that through the resurrection of Jesus and the events that it triggered God is bringing a new humanity into existence. Israel, on the other hand, having pursued a "Law of righteousness"—that is, the righteousness that comes through diligent and consistent communal adherence to the statutes and commandments—has failed to achieve it. They have stumbled over the stumbling stone: "Behold, I am laying in Zion a stone of stumbling, and a rock of offense; and whoever believes in him will not be put to shame" (Rom 9:33). Two passages from Isaiah are fused together in the quotation. In the first, it is YHWH himself who is "a stone of offense and a rock of stumbling to both houses of Israel, a trap and a snare to the inhabitants of Jerusalem. And many shall stumble upon it" (Isa 8:14–15). Because Israel has been disobedient and has not feared the Lord, God will be in their midst as a destructive force. In the second passage, the "scoffers, who rule this people in Jerusalem," believe that they have made a pact with death, that it will not touch them; but they are badly mistaken: "your covenant with death will be annulled, and your agreement with Sheol will not stand; when the overwhelming scourge passes through, you will be beaten down by it" (28:18). Isaiah has "heard a decree of destruction from the Lord God of hosts against the whole land" (28:22). But a stone has been laid as a foundation in Jerusalem, and "the one who believes in him will not be put to shame" (28:14–16). Paul has fused into this single image the thought of God as judge of his people and the thought of Jesus as the foundation of a reconstructed people. Those who believe in him "will not be put to shame": they will live, they will survive, they will be vindicated.

The Righteousness That Is from Faith(fulness): 10:1-21

So we must imagine Paul in intense, impassioned dispute with his own people about the implications of their refusal to accept that Jesus's death and resurrection constitute in any sense a way of salvation for Israel. He believes that destruction is decreed, that time is running out, that the leaders of the people are culpably complacent, and that for all their renowned zeal for the Law, they have failed to grasp the fact that history is moving—or is being moved—towards a turning point that is beyond the reach of the Law, when God will establish his own righteousness on his own terms. The Jews have failed to demonstrate a righteousness in the world, a concrete moral and spiritual integrity by which their God might be vindicated against the gods of the nations—on the contrary, they have discredited him (cf. 2:24). So God is bringing the long narrative of the Law to a close or to a climax[2] by establishing an alternative righteousness for everyone who believes; and this, Paul argues, will provide the basis on which the *oikoumenē* will change its mind.

What follows in 10:5–21 is a rewriting of Deuteronomy 30:11–14. Wright makes much of the "exilic" context of this passage.[3] It is preceded by an account (Deut 30:1–10) of how God will restore his scattered people from the "uttermost parts of heaven" if they will call to mind the blessing and the curse and repent and return to the Lord to obey his voice. But there are reasons to doubt that this was at the forefront of Paul's mind.

2. See Wright, *Romans*, 655–58, for discussion of the meaning of *telos* here.

3. Wright, *Romans*, 658–64.

First, the emphasis in Deuteronomy 30:11–14 is on the accessibility of the commandment "today," not *after* the exile. It belongs with the subsequent paragraph: "See, I have set before you today life and good, death and evil . . ." (30:15). Secondly, for Paul the day of God's wrath against Israel—a judgment analogous to the disaster of the Babylonian invasion—lies in the future. He rewrites Deuteronomy 30:11–14 in order to show how easy it would be for Jews *now* to believe, call upon the name of the Lord, and so be saved from this future destruction (Rom 10:9–13). It is true, thirdly, that he casts himself in the role of Isaiah's messenger, who announces good things to the people in exile (10:15–16). But if geography is indeed relevant here, it is likely, given the context, that it has more to do with Paul taking the gospel to the Jews and Gentiles of the *oikoumenē* than with Israel returning from exile. Finally, the quotations of Romans 10:19–21 evoke a pre-judgment rather than a post-judgment setting. When Israel provokes God to anger with their idols, he will "make them jealous with those who are no people," he will "provoke them to anger with a foolish nation," and then he will "heap disasters upon them" (Deut 32:21, 23). Isaiah speaks of God spreading out his hands "all the day to a rebellious people," a people who provoke him with their strange idolatrous practices, who will therefore be punished for their iniquities—and he is bold enough to imagine God making himself available to people who do not ask for him or seek him, to "a nation that was not called by my name" (Isa 65:1–7).

So we may now restate Paul's argument here. There is a "righteousness which is from the Law" that can be summed up in the words of Moses from Leviticus 18:5: "You shall therefore keep my statutes and my rules; if a person does them, he shall live by them." Paul's message has been that this ideal of national life has proved unattainable and, because of wrath, has been superseded by the Habakkuk principle, which is that the "righteous shall live by faithfulness." For Paul, of course, as for both Moses and Habakkuk, "life" signifies neither personal spiritual well-being nor a heavenly post-mortem existence but the survival and prosperity and blessing of the Jews as a distinct chosen people, his kinsmen according to the flesh (9:3). But the "righteousness from faithfulness" speaks quite differently to the "righteousness which is from the Law." It creatively, even playfully, and therefore inexactly, rewrites the biblical text of Deuteronomy 30:11–14. There is no need to ascend into heaven to bring

Christ down, or into the abyss to bring Christ up from the dead. The word of faith(fulness) by which a people may live during a time of wrath is immediately accessible: "if you confess with your mouth that Jesus is Lord and believe in your heart that God raised him from the dead, you will be saved" (10:9). Moreover, because God is Lord of all and will judge not only Israel but also the *oikoumenē*, it is as true for Greeks as it is for Jews that those who believe in the one who has proven to be a stone of stumbling for Israel will not be put to shame (10:11; cf. 9:33), and that those who call on the name of the Lord will be saved (cf. Joel 2:32). But that is by way of a parenthesis. Paul's overriding interest here is in the response of his fellow Jews. The good news of what God has done for his people has been announced to them, but they have not believed what was said about a servant who was wounded because of Israel's transgressions, crushed because of Israel's iniquities, punished so that Israel might find healing and peace (10:16; cf. Isa 53:1–5). Word of it has gone out to all the earth and to the ends of the Greco-Roman *oikoumenē*. But Israel has not understood (10:19).

Has God Rejected His people? 11:1–35

A man at the back of the synagogue shouts out, "So what are you saying? That God has rejected us, his people?" There are murmurings. "Not at all," Paul answers. "I am a Jew, an Israelite, from the seed of Abraham, of the tribe of Benjamin. But you tell me, what does the Scripture say about Elijah, when he complains that the idolatrous people of Israel have thrown down the altars of YHWH and killed the prophets, and that he alone is left? Do you remember how God answered him? 'I have kept for myself seven thousand men who have not bowed the knee to Baal' (Rom 11:4; cf. 1 Kings 19:9–18). Well, we have the same situation now: 'there is a remnant, chosen by grace' (Rom 11:5)."

"But what about the rest of us?" The man indicates with a sweep of his arm those gathered in the room. "What about those of us who are not convinced that your Jesus is the Christ?" We may imagine Paul hesitating before he responds, trying to assess the mood of his audience. "I will tell you what I believe. You are like those who succumbed to a spirit of stupor before the armies of the nations came to fight against Mount Zion. You have eyes that do not see, ears that do not hear—your prophets and seers are oblivious to what is happening (Rom 11:8; cf. Deut 29:4; Isa 29:10; 43:8). You are like those who opposed David, of whom he said, 'Let their table become a snare and a trap, a stumbling block and a retribution for them; let their eyes be darkened so that they cannot see, and bend their backs forever' (Ps 69:22–23). You are blind to the destruction that is about to come upon our people."

At this several voices are raised in protest. "Listen to me!" Paul shouts against the growing hubbub. "It is my heart's desire—God knows—that all Israel should be saved from the wrath that is coming upon this world. But you have to understand this. God is not beholden to us just because we are Jews, just because we have the Law, just because we are not like the unclean Gentiles. We cannot expect to stand in his way if now at last he has chosen to demonstrate his righteousness to the nations. We cannot complain if the Lord of all and Judge of all has called not only Jews but also Gentiles as a clear sign that he will not stay forever marginalized by the so-called gods of this world and misrepresented by a wicked and adulterous people, who worship him with their lips but whose hearts are . . ."

What follows is perhaps a sharp and intemperate altercation that ends with Paul and his companions being dragged out into the streets by a mob of angry Jews. Not for the first time, they are lucky to escape with their lives. Paul must have had doubts, as they made their way bruised and frustrated to the home of friends, that these people would ever be made jealous by the inclusion of the nations in the purposes of God (cf. Acts 13:44–52); but he would not give up on the hope, not yet: "if their trespass means riches for the world, and if their failure means riches for the Gentiles, how much more will their full inclusion mean!" (11:12). The word translated "failure" here (*hēttēma*) would normally mean "defeat," in particular military defeat.[4] It may be, therefore, that Paul is thinking of the foreseen defeat of the Jews by the Romans, which comes as a consequence of their habitual trespass against the Law. This would suggest that in his mind, if there is to be a "full inclusion" (*plērōma*) of Israel, it will come after, rather than before, the destruction of Jerusalem and the temple. I will argue that this is also the scenario that Paul has in mind in 11:26 when he speaks of the salvation of "all Israel."

---

4. The noun is found in the LXX only at Isa 31:8, where it is used for the "defeat" of the Assyrians. The verb *hēttaō* is common in LXX and Josephus with the sense "overcome" or "defeat."

Now that the place of the nations in the scheme of things has been brought firmly into view, he addresses himself directly to the Gentiles in Rome in order to highlight for them the implications of his argument about Israel (11:13). There is clearly some concern here that the incoming Gentile believers may prematurely displace and disenfranchise the ab-original Jewish-Christian communities. They must not think too highly of themselves. They must not get carried away with their newfound status. Perhaps Paul is beginning to be alarmed by the success of his mission. He has deliberately played up his service to the Gentiles in order to provoke the Jews—in the hope of shaking some of them at least out of their com-placency in the short period of time that is left before the day of wrath comes (11:13–14). Their rejection has led to the reconciliation of Gentiles to the God of Israel, but the swing in the direction of the nations can still be reversed, and that will mean "life from the dead"—the restoration of Israel *following judgment* (cf. Dan 12:2–3; Hos 6:1–2). [Again we have a hint that Paul expects a national return to God to happen—if it is going to happen at all—immediately *after the coming judgment.*]

For now, at least, it remains the case that the whole lump of the dough of Israel is not less holy than the portion that is consecrated as firstfruits, and the branches are not less holy than the stem. Yes, Paul will admit a few verses later, the majority of Jews have become enemies of God, and the Gentile Christians in Rome have benefited from that. But "as regards elec-tion, they are beloved for the sake of their forefathers" (11:28). They have rebelled and they face judgment, but "the gifts and the calling of God are irrevocable"; and the possibility remains that God will have mercy upon them (11:31–32). The firstfruits are the "remnant chosen by grace," called, presumably, not only from Jews but also from Gentiles (9:24; 11:5). The sacrificial aspect is of incidental significance here, but it will be picked up at the beginning of chapter 12 when Paul calls the community of firstfruits in Rome to present their bodies "as a living sacrifice, holy and acceptable to God." The root of the olive tree cannot be the remnant because even Jewish Christians must remain connected by grace. It is also unlikely to be Christ since it would make no sense to accuse the grafted-in Gentiles of thinking that they "support the root" (11:18). Most likely, then, the statement "if the root is holy, so are the branches" corresponds to the later argument that "as regards election, they are beloved for the sake of their forefathers" (11:28): the root that in some sense ensures the holiness even of a disobedient people is the patriarchs.[5] At this stage, therefore, ten years before the outbreak of war, Paul can claim that, on account of both the small number of believing Jews and the promise to the fathers, Israel is still important to God, perhaps still central to his purposes. But that does not preclude judgment, and as we shall see, it will very much depend on how Israel responds to judgment.

The Gentiles are branches of a wild olive that have been grafted into the tree of Israel in order to share in the "root of the richness (*tēs rhizēs tēs piotētos*) of the olive tree": they have come to have a stake in the promise that the descendants of Abraham will inherit the world. But they must be careful not to "boast over the branches" (11:18, my translation). There is no ground for contempt towards the Jews. If they take the kindness of God for granted, they are likely to be cut off again. To this extent there is some force to Elliott's otherwise overstated, over-anxious, and historically misplaced endeavor to turn Paul's argument against Israel on its head and shift all blame on to the arrogant nations. We may well have here the first signs of the radical re-appropriation of an essentially Jewish identity that became Christendom—"the reflex, within the Christ assemblies, of the arrogance of empire, which regards the imperial disposition of the destinies of peoples as the climax of history."[6] At the same time, if the Jews do not continue in unbelief, they will be grafted back in, "for God has the power to graft them in again" (11:23). Paul entertains the possibility that the many Jews who have refused to accept the "gospel of God"—not simply the offer of personal salvation and eternal life but the warning of a coming judgment and the invitation to find a way of national survival along a path defined by Jesus—may be reinstated *on condition that "they do not continue in their unbelief."*

It is important for Paul that his readers in Rome get this clear in their minds: the inclusion of Gentiles is both contingent upon and instrumental in what God is doing with Israel. They are a means to an end. Israel has been "hardened" *in part* (cf. 11:7) for the sake of the *ecumenical—oikoumenē*-wide—vindication of God; branches have been broken off in order that the family of Abraham may be internationalized and inherit the world. This is the "mystery" that has been disclosed in this largely unexpected turn of events. But the hope remains that when

5. Cf. Dunn, *Romans 9–16*, 658–59.

6. Elliott, *Arrogance*, 110.

sufficient Gentiles have come in, Israel will be fully restored to God—if not because of jealousy that Gentiles have come to share in the rich root of the patriarchs, then in the manner suggested by the quotations from Isaiah: "'The Deliverer will come from Zion, he will banish ungodliness from Jacob'; 'and this will be my covenant with them when I take away their sins'" (11:26).

The restoration that Isaiah envisages, however, comes *as a consequence of judgment*. God sees the lawlessness of Israel: "Justice is turned back, and righteousness stands far away; for truth has stumbled in the public squares, and uprightness cannot enter" (Isa 59:14); and since there is no one to intercede and put matters right, God will intervene directly, arming himself with righteousness and salvation, clothing himself with vengeance and zeal; and he will execute judgment: "According to their deeds, so will he repay, wrath to his adversaries, repayment to his enemies" (59:18). The deliverer will come "for the sake of Zion, and he will turn away impiety from Jacob" (59:20 LXX, my translation); and God will make a covenant with them, that the Spirit that is upon his servant and the words that are in his mouth will not fail (59:21). Paul has modified the last part by merging it with Isaiah 27:9 LXX: "Because of this the lawlessness of Jacob will be removed, and this is his blessing, when I remove his sin . . ." (my translation). But the important thought to extract from this narrative is that salvation will take place *after* YHWH has come in wrath to banish unrighteousness and impiety from Zion. Isaiah 60:10 encapsulates the order of things: "in my wrath I struck you, but in my favor I have had mercy on you" (cf. Dan 9:11–19).

Paul does not expect Israel as a nation to escape destruction—the most he can do for now, as apostle to the nations, is attempt to provoke some Jews to jealousy in the hope that they will be reconciled to the God who is boldly rewriting the storyline for the sake of the future of his people. But he has seen in Isaiah the possibility that having been punished, having been devastated by the invading armies of Rome, Israel will return *as a people* to YHWH and be forgiven and be restored.[7] Then, when the

---

7. According to Dunn, *Romans 9–16*, 681, there is now a "strong consensus" that *pas Israēl* must mean "Israel as a whole, as a people whose corporate identity and wholeness would not be lost even if in the event there were some (or indeed many) individual exceptions." Wright disagrees: his view is that "all Israel" denotes "the whole family of Abraham, Jew and Gentile alike," who will be saved "during the course of present history" through "their coming to Christian faith" (Wright, *Romans*, 689).

earth is in darkness, the Lord will arise upon them; the scattered sons and daughters of the diaspora will come back to the land; nations will come to their light, bringing their wealth with them in tribute, even transporting the exiles home; foreigners will rebuild the razed walls of Jerusalem, and kings will serve them; the temple will be decorated again with timber from Lebanon; the days of mourning will be over, and YHWH will be an everlasting light in their midst (Isa 60:1–22). I suggest that Paul has drawn from this continuation of the text that he quotes a fully realistic hope for the transformed historical existence of national Israel under a new covenant in the Spirit.

The decisive condition inserted in 11:23, however, remains in force: "if they do not continue in their unbelief . . ." The Jews will be grafted in again to the tree and will share in the inheritance promised to Abraham *if* they come to understand and believe that judgment and restoration for this people have been preempted in Jesus, who has been made Lord and judge of all. To make sense of Paul's argument, therefore, we need to read 11:25 as a parenthesis in which he clarifies his central point of concern in addressing the Gentiles directly: Jewish recalcitrance has led to the inclusion of the nations, but this is not yet to be thought of as an unrestrained or wholesale displacement of Israel. Some sort of limit has been set to the number of Gentiles that will come in before the wrath of God takes effect. It is still only a means to a possible end. If we bracket the verse in this way, the argument runs smoothly from verse 24 to verse 26: if Gentiles from a wild olive tree can be grafted in to Israel, there will hardly be a problem in re-attaching the original branches that were cut off because of disobedience; and in this way all Israel will be saved—not only the remnant but also that larger part of Israel that currently stands under judgment and faces the destruction of AD 70.

This reading also avoids—rather elegantly, it seems to me—the exegetical and theological difficulties that arise if we suppose that the salvation of all Israel is made somehow directly and almost mechanically dependent on the inclusion of a sufficient number of Gentiles in the people of God. It resolves the contradiction with the condition that is inserted in 11:23. We can give due weight to the fact that Paul appears *not* to have expected "all Israel" to be made jealous by the inclusion of Gentiles (11:14). We do not have to posit "a large-scale salvation of ethnic Jews" at the end of time, a doctrine that Wright is so keen to avoid not least because such a gratuitous salvation seems completely at odds with the argument so far: "If Paul has indeed, while writing the letter, received as some have suggested a fresh revelation to the effect that the whole Jewish race will at the last be saved by some special means, he did the wrong thing by adding it to what he had already written."[8]

As things turned out, Israel did not repent in the way that Paul hoped following the traumatic events of AD 66–73. Texts such as 2 *Baruch* and 4 *Ezra* show that post-war Judaism could interpret the destruction of Jerusalem and the temple as punishment for Israel's sins, going so far as to agree with Paul that the Law could not bring forth fruit because God did not take away from the descendants of Abraham the "evil heart" that had been transmitted to them from Adam. Sacrifices were offered in the temple for many years, but in the end "the inhabitants of the city transgressed, in everything doing as Adam and all his descendants had done"; so God delivered the city into the hands of their enemies (4 *Ezra* 3.20–27). We hear the admission that the Jews have acted in ways that bring death, that they have "no works of righteousness, that all have acted wickedly, all have transgressed"—and precisely in this the righteousness and goodness of God will be declared, "when you are merciful to those who have no store of good works" (4 *Ezra* 8.31–36). But there is no acknowledgement that Jesus was right in his condemnation of Israel or that God has indeed made him Lord and Christ by raising him from the dead; there is no embrace of the Gentiles as a sign that God claims sovereignty over the whole earth. So the center of gravity shifts, and we find ourselves moving rapidly in the direction of a people uprooted from Jewish soil and eventually replanted in the very different cultural and intellectual environment of the Greco-Roman world, where, of course, it flourished and became a great overarching tree, and the birds of the air came and made their nests in its branches—not quite what Jesus had in mind, perhaps, but not an altogether unreasonable extrapolation from his parable (Matt 13:31–32 and parallels).

8. Wright, *Romans*, 689.

12

The Formation of an Eschatological Community

Paul concludes the lengthy recapitulation of the argument that he has developed over the years in his work as an apostle, from Jerusalem round to Illyricum, with a doxology (11:33–36), in which he invokes Isaiah 40:13: "Who has measured the Spirit of the Lord, or what man shows him his counsel?" Jerusalem is the herald of good news who is told to say to the cities of Judah that the Lord comes with might, that "his arm rules for him; behold, his reward is with him, and his recompense before him." In this he is absolutely sovereign: no one has advised him; no one has taught him knowledge or shown him the way of understanding. The nations are too small to defy him: they are like a drop from a bucket, dust that is too light to affect the balance of the scales; they are "as nothing before him." He sits above the circle of the earth, looking down on its insect-like inhabitants; he "brings princes to nothing, and makes the rulers of the earth as emptiness" (Isa 40:9–23). The passage gives resonant narrative amplification to Paul's conviction that God has raised Jesus from the dead and appointed him as judge—of Israel first, then of the nations—and that the time will come when the persecuted saints of the Most High will inherit the world that is currently under the sway of despotic, destructive powers. This is the work of a God whose judgments and ways are beyond human understanding.

The believers in Rome have bought into this narrative through their baptism into the death and life of Jesus: they are "called to belong to Jesus Christ," they are called to be "saints," called to suffer with him in order that they may be glorified with him—for the sake of the future of the

139

people of God (Rom 1:6–7; 8:17). If that is the essential orientation of their vocation under clearly defined eschatological conditions, with the trauma of divine judgment on the horizon, we must naturally consider to what extent Paul's plea to the brethren to "present your bodies as a living sacrifice" (12:1) and the ensuing instructions about community life have been determined—and delimited—by this specific argument.

He makes it quite clear that a primary reason for writing to the saints in Rome was to ensure that the "offering of the nations might be acceptable" (15:16). The figure may be multifaceted: there is perhaps an allusion to Isaiah 66:20 LXX and the image of the Gentiles bringing the scattered Jews to Jerusalem "as a gift to the Lord"; and there may be the thought that this offering of the nations is tangibly represented by the collection taken from the churches of the *oikoumenē* for the "poor among the saints in Jerusalem" (15:26–27). But this acceptable offering must also recall the appeal that stands at the head of the whole section that the brothers and sisters in Rome should present their bodies "as a living sacrifice, holy and acceptable to God, which is your spiritual worship" (12:1). Against the background chatter of Hellenistic Judaism the metaphor is likely to have been interpreted eschatologically. Wisdom of Solomon, as was noted with reference to Romans 8:3, speaks of the persecution and killing of the righteous in similar terms. To all appearances they were being punished for a crime, but in reality they were being disciplined and tested by God, who has accepted them as "a sacrificial whole burnt offering"; and they will come to share in the resurrection that will mark the restoration of the people of God and the coming rule over the nations (Wis 3:1–8). Paul regarded his own suffering (and eventually his impending execution) as a libation that was being poured out over the sacrifice and service of the Philippians' faith (Phil 2:17; cf. 2 Tim 4:6).

So he writes to the churches in Rome in order that they may understand fully what it means to have been written into a narrative of momentous social and religious transformation that will culminate in the transference of sovereignty over the nations from the manifold gods of the present age to Jesus Christ, who has been appointed Son of God in power by his resurrection from the dead. This is the premise for a good part—and in some sense for all—of the practical parenetic material in Paul's Letters: he teaches the churches how to hold together as communities, how to love and support one another, how to remain faithful to their calling, how to relate to outsiders, *while travelling Jesus's narrow and difficult road leading to life.* I suggest, in particular, that it is the premise for the metaphor that he develops in 1 Corinthians 3:10–15 of the church as a building—perhaps even as a temple—that will be subjected to fire on a day of testing. This is Paul's version of Jesus's story about the impact of the storm and flood of divine judgment on two houses, one built unwisely on sand, the other built on rock (Matt 7:24–27), which, in turn, is Jesus's version of Ezekiel's story about a white-washed wall that is swept away in a storm on a day of wrath against Jerusalem (Ezek 13:10–16).[1] Paul's Day of Fire is not a final judgment: it is the time of social upheaval and distress that he foresees in 1 Corinthians 7:26–31; it is the persecution that the churches of the *oikoumenē* will face in the coming years. In the first place, therefore, the churches must be built on the foundation of Jesus Christ, who suffered and was vindicated. But even then, if the community has been constructed from worthless, flammable materials, it will be destroyed in the conflagration: it will not survive the persecution. Only churches constructed from costly, fire-resistant materials will still be standing after the "form of this world" has passed away (1 Cor 7:31). The apostles, therefore, will be judged and rewarded at the *parousia*, when Christ is publicly vindicated, *according to this basic eschatological criterion*: did they build and support resilient communities that would survive the coming testing of persecution? This is at the heart of Paul's motivation as an apostle (cf. 2 Cor 1:14; Phil 3:17—4:1; 1 Thess 2:19; 3:11–13; 2 Thess 1:4).

The Night Is Far Gone, the Day Is at Hand: 13:11–14

As modern interpreters we are accustomed to making allowances for Paul's occasional apocalyptic aberrations, when he departs from his usually sane theologizing and momentarily—and surely inadvertently—channels one of the maniacal spirits of Jewish end-time speculation. We have just such a lapse in good form in Romans 13:11–14: the night is far gone, the day is at hand, and "salvation is nearer to us now than when we first believed." We charitably put this apparent miscalculation down to an excitable temperament; or perhaps we credit Paul with a subtle existentialist sensibility that feels the weight of the ultimate to be always pressing in upon the

1. See Perriman, *Re: Mission*, 44–45.

present. But the reading of Romans that we have pursued to this point has made it clear that his sense of eschatological urgency should be taken at face value: it is time for the community of saints in Rome to wake from sleep and face up to the harsh realities of their future.

Traditional interpretation of this passage, being reluctant to take consistent account of the eschatological structure of Paul's thought, has muddled up night and day. The controlling metaphor is a military one: the saints are thought of as soldiers *before a day of battle*; Paul is the general who walks from tent to tent in the gloom before dawn, rousing his men from their sleep—throwing a bucket of cold water over their heads if necessary—and urging them to prepare for the conflict that lies ahead.

We find the same imagery—and the same argument—in two other texts. Paul warns the Thessalonians that the *day* of the Lord will come unexpectedly, as birth pains come upon a pregnant woman, bringing sudden destruction. They are prepared for this: they do not belong to this time of illusory "peace and security"; they are not asleep or drunk during this long night of waiting; they are already "sons of light and sons of the day." They have been called precisely for this purpose; it is the story that they find themselves in. So they must now put on the protective armor that they will need when the "day of God's wrath" comes: the breastplate of faith and love, the helmet of the hope that they will be saved from destruction. This is how they will overcome persecution: by trusting in God, by loving one another at all costs, knowing that Jesus "died for us so that . . . we might live with him" (1 Thess 5:1–11).

In similar fashion, presupposing the same martyrological narrative, he exhorts the Ephesians, who have been "predestined . . . for adoption as sons of God" (Eph 1:5), to be "imitators of God, as beloved children"; they are to love in the way that Christ loved—that is, they are to give themselves up willingly as an "offering and sacrifice (*thysian*) to God"; they are to put their lives on the line (5:1–2). They are to leave behind all manner of idolatry and immorality—the behaviors of a passing age, which will bring the wrath of God upon the "sons of disobedience" (5:6; cf. 2:3). They are to leave behind darkness and walk in the light; they are to "awake . . . and rise from the dead"; they are to walk carefully in the light "because the days are evil" (5:7–16). Finally, they are to put on the "armor of God" so that they may be able to resist the schemes of the devil and stand fast "in the day of evil," when they will find themselves assaulted by the ferocious spiritual powers that move darkly behind the political institutions of flesh and blood (6:10–16). The parenesis is oriented towards an eschatological event—a "day of evil," a "day of redemption" for which they have been sealed (4:30).

When Paul tells the Romans, therefore, that it is time to wake from sleep, that "salvation is nearer to us than when we first believed," that the night is far gone and the day is at hand, that they should "put on the weapons of light," that they should "walk properly as in the day," that they should "make no provision for the desires of the flesh" (Rom 13:11–14), he means that a day of persecution is approaching from which they will be "saved" by putting on the armor of a sober and righteous lifestyle. The coming of the day does not bring an end to trouble: "night" in this metaphorical schema is not simply the "present evil age" (cf. Gal 1:4) that will eventually be replaced by a wonderful heavenly daytime.[2] On the contrary, night is a time of false peace and security, the lull before the storm; the coming of the day marks the *beginning* of trouble, which is why, like soldiers before a battle, they must wake from sleep—or abandon unseemly practices that belong to the night—and put on the armor that will protect them in a time of severe conflict. They are to "put on Christ" (13:14; cf. Col 3:12) for the same purpose—not because that is what it means to be Christian but because it is only by identifying with the one who was brutally killed and who was vindicated, by being built on the foundation of Jesus Christ, that the community will survive the coming day of wrath.

In less than a decade many of the saints in Rome, whom Paul was so anxious to visit and encourage, some of whom he probably knew personally (cf. Rom 16:3–15), would be rounded up without warning at the whim of a desperate emperor, charged with the crime of being Christian, and subjected to appalling punishments. The night of complacency was over; the day had begun. Interpretation does not require us to think that Paul had anything more than a vague but compelling premonition of what lay ahead for the churches of the *oikoumenē*, or that he had any detailed notion of the actual protracted and sporadic form that systemic pagan opposition to the renewed, multinational people of God would

---

2. Against, e.g., Moo, *Romans*, 821. If "day" here has "a very positive overtone in contrast to 'night'" (Dunn, *Romans 9–16*, 787), it makes no sense for Paul to urge his readers to put on armor.

take. He uses more or less generic prophetic and apocalyptic language to give narrative form to certain unshakeable convictions regarding the future of communities that associated themselves with the man in whose name God would judge the established order of things. The challenge we now face as readers is to situate ourselves imaginatively in the same time and place, at the dangerous margins of an antipathetic culture, with the voices of Scripture and of first-century Judaism ringing in our ears, and with the vision impressed in our minds of a risen Lord who embraces in himself the persecuted community, and then to consider how the future might appear from that restricted but potent perspective.

Do Not Be Overcome by Evil

In Romans 12:1—15:7 Paul sets out not merely a "new way for all to respond to God's grace"[3] but what it means for the saints in Rome to be prepared for the struggle that lies ahead. If they are to be a genuinely sacrificial community, willing to participate actively in the story of Jesus's death and resurrection, they cannot afford to remain "conformed *to this age*" (12:2)—the temporal, and therefore historical, aspect to the exhortation is lost when *tō aiōni toutō* is translated "this world." Their whole way of thinking must be changed if they are to make the arduous journey from their old lives under the Jewish Law or under the pagan gods to an eventual public, political-religious vindication and the life of the age to come, when a just, Spirit-filled people of God, under the lordship of the one who has been given the name which is above every name, will represent in its life and in its proclamation the sovereign presence of the God of Abraham across the face of a radically transformed *oikoumenē*.

This will require, in the first place, a selflessness that has regard for the interests and value of others in the community. This is a central plank of Paul's eschatologically oriented parenesis. For example, he urges the Philippians not to be frightened by their opponents because "it has been granted to you that for the sake of Christ you should not only believe in him but also suffer for his sake." In view of this they must be of one mind, having the same love; they must not act out of rivalry or vanity but must put the interests of others in the community above their own; they must, in a nutshell, have the mind and attitude of Christ Jesus, who

3. Witherington and Hyatt, *Romans*, 59.

made himself of no account, endured humiliation and physical suffering, and was killed, all the while trusting that God would vindicate him (Phil 1:29—2:11). This is what it meant in practice for their "manner of life" to be "worthy of the gospel of Christ" (Phil 1:27). Like the saints in Rome, they have been called not merely to be saved but to participate directly in the story of Jesus—a story which, as becomes apparent in chapter 3, Paul was eager to replicate in his own life.

So the saints in Rome should not think too highly of themselves: rather, they are a body in Christ, a community constituted by the story of Christ, in which they are "individually members one of another." The eschatological aspect of this metaphor has not always been recognized. Although it is used principally to moderate the tensions generated by charismatic gifting, the argument in 1 Corinthians 12:12–27 concludes with the statement: "If one member suffers, all the members suffer together (*sympaschei*); if one member is glorified (*doxazetai*), all the members rejoice together" (12:26, my translation). If Paul had in mind the mutual *honoring* of members of the community, as is usually supposed, *timaō* would have been the obvious choice (cf. Rom 12:10; 1 Cor 12:23–24; Eph 6:21; 1 Tim 5:3; 6:1). The only other place where Paul uses the verbs *sympaschō* and (*syn*)*doxazō*, together or separately, with reference to the believer is in Romans 8:17, 30: those who *suffer together* with Christ will be *glorified together* with Christ. This strongly suggests an eschatological focus for the argument: it is as a mutually supportive body that they will overcome opposition and hardship. In Ephesians the body is the fullness of Christ, who was raised from the dead and seated at the right hand of God, "far above all rule and authority and power and dominion, and above every name that is named, not only in this age but also in the one to come" (Eph 1:21–22). The body is a charismatic community, gifted by Christ when he ascended on high, which must "attain to the unity of the faith and of the knowledge of the Son of God, to mature manhood, to the measure of the stature of the fullness of Christ" (4:13) if it is not to be seduced from its calling—ultimately, when the "evil day" of persecution comes (6:13). In Colossians to "hold fast to the Head" is to remain true to their identity as a community that has died and been raised with Christ and has its mind set on the glory that will be revealed when the wrath of God comes and Jesus is publicly acknowledged in the world (Col 2:20—3:6). These familiar pictures of the relationship between Christ and the churches do not require a great deal of digital enhancement in order to discern in them the thought that the communities of saints constitute living, eschatologically significant embodiments of the story of Jesus's suffering and vindication.

In any case, the continuation of the argument in Romans 12 brings the eschatological premise sharply into focus. Rejoice in the hope of vindication for which you have been prepared by your suffering, Paul tells them (cf. 5:2–5); be patient in the tribulation that will accompany the day of wrath (cf. 2:9; 5:3; 8:35); and be constant in prayer—like the abused widow in Jesus's parable about eschatological prayer, who persisted in seeking justice against her adversary (Luke 18:1–5). "And will not God give justice to his elect, who cry to him day and night? Will he delay long over them? I tell you, he will give justice to them speedily. Nevertheless, when the Son of Man comes, will he find faith on earth?" (18:7–8). The saints in Rome are not to seek vengeance against their enemies but are to bless those who persecute them; they are to feed them if they are hungry, give them something to drink if they are thirsty; they are to overcome evil by means of good, for vengeance should be left to the wrath of God: "Vengeance is mine, I will repay, says the Lord" (Rom 12:14–21). The allusion is not inadvertent or mindless of its origins: the Song of Moses describes the evils that God in his anger will heap upon a perverse and faithless generation of Israelites; this judgment is stored up and its time will come, because "Vengeance is mine, and recompense, for the time when their foot shall slip; for the day of their calamity is at hand, and their doom comes swiftly" (Deut 32:35; cf. Lev 19:18). They do not need to seek revenge because the day is coming when God himself will overthrow their enemies—both the Jew, first, and the Greek; both faithless Jerusalem and the lawless *oikoumenē*.

Between the insistence that the saints in Rome should never avenge themselves against their persecutors but "give opportunity" for the wrath of God and the warning that the day of battle is not far away, we have the controversial passage about submission to governing authorities (13:1–7) and a brief paragraph about love being the fulfillment of the Law (13:8–10). Like many commentators, Elliott has concluded that the tensions between this passage and Paul's anti-imperial apocalypticism are irresolvable. They "arise, not from an idiosyncratic incoherence on Paul's part, but from fundamentally irresolvable contradictions in the material and ideological conditions in which the letter was written and which the letter was an attempt to resolve."[4] He admits, however, that he finds compelling the argument that Paul's teaching here must be understood in the light of reports that may have implicated Jews in anti-government agitation, and it is unclear why he does not pursue this line of thought further.[5]

Commonly in Jewish literature when nations are reminded that their authority has been ordained by God, it is because they have exceeded that authority specifically by threatening and oppressing Israel (e.g., 1 Macc 4:10–12; 2 Bar. 82.1–9). The language of opposition and resistance in 13:2 (*antitassomenos . . . anthestēken . . . anthestēkotes*) suggests that what Paul has in mind here is not merely unlawful behavior but some more active form of insubordination or defiance.[6] Josephus uses *antitassō* for the opposition of the Jews to the command that images of Caesar should be placed in the cities of Israel, describing their attitude as tantamount to rebellion (Josephus *J.W.* 2.194).[7] Similarly, for the sake of the preservation of the sanctuary Simon son of Mattathias and his brothers "gave themselves to danger and resisted (*antestēsan*) those opposing their nation" (1 Macc 14:29, my translation). We may conjecture, then, that Paul is concerned that Jewish Christians in Rome or elsewhere, and perhaps Gentile believers along with them, might be caught up in the sort of militant Jewish unruliness that would eventually bring destruction upon the nation. This would explain why in wielding the sword Rome plays the part of the "servant of God, an avenger who carries out God's wrath on the wrongdoer" (13:4). Wrath against the rebellious Jew, first, is by the hand of the powers that be, appointed by God for that purpose, whether that is in the form of the destruction of Jerusalem or through the suppression of Jewish unrest across the empire.

Paul's counter-strategy is not merely that they should avoid a dangerous provocation of the pagan state: they should actively "do what is

---

4. Elliott, *Arrogance*, 156.

5. Ibid., 154.

6. Dunn, *Romans 9–16*, 762, notes that *anthistēmi* is typically used in the LXX "for a resistance which is unavailing before superior strength." Note Wright, *Romans*, 623, on growing provocation and unrest in Judea.

7. The word generally carries connotations of rebellion and military opposition in Josephus: *Ant.* 4.300; 13.94; 19.252; *J.W.* 3.15, 500; 4.132; he has Caesar address the Roman army, speaking of the "rash boldness and brutish rage of their [Jewish] antagonists (*antitetagmenōn*)" (*J.W.* 7.7).

good," blessing those who persecute them, as far as possible being at peace with all people, overcoming evil with good (12:14–21). This is the point of the paragraph about love, which otherwise seems out of place. If, out of what Paul now regards as a profoundly misplaced zeal for the Law (cf. Phil 3:4–7), Jews both in Judea and across the *oikoumenē* were disposed towards violent resistance, Paul's argument is that what the Law fundamentally enjoins is an attitude of love that expresses itself concretely and socially in the payment of taxes, revenue, respect, and honor where these things are owed (13:6–7). The significance of this for the future of the churches can be shown from Eusebius. He records, for example, the official ambivalence regarding the justness of the persecutions, famously illustrated by the letter of Pliny the Younger to Trajan. Citing Tertullian's summary of the exchange, Eusebius emphasizes the fact that Trajan could find "nothing wicked in their behaviour, other than their unwillingness to worship idols." The Christians upheld their teaching by "forbidding murder, adultery, fraud, robbery, and the like," in view of which Trajan mitigated state policy against the church (Eusebius *Hist. eccl.* 3.33.1–4). The letter from the Gallic churches relates how a woman called Blandina "found comfort for her sufferings by saying, 'I am a Christian, and nothing wicked happens among us'" (5.1.19).

Finally, the teaching in 14:1—15:6 about those who are weak and strong in faith also lends itself to an eschatologically oriented reappraisal. The issue here is not merely the practical task of persuading Jewish and Gentile believers to get along with each other, even if the problems created by the expulsion of the Jews from Rome in AD 49 and their return following Claudius's death are somewhere in the background. The issue is framed by the question of whether they will stand or fall when they face the judgment of eschatological crisis, when God judges the ancient world on account of its idolatry, when every knee shall bow and every tongue will give praise to God (14:10–12). As so often in his letters, Paul's practical teaching has in view the need to instill in his communities a corporate character that will survive the fires of persecution. In light of this coming testing of the faith of the community, there is very little to be gained from petty internal disputes over dietary restrictions and feast days.

The section concludes with a last appeal to the controlling story of Jesus. Those who are powerful have an obligation to bear with the weaknesses of the powerless; the community will fail if everyone looks to his own interests; each of them should seek to please his neighbor for his good—to build him up. That is what Christ did. He did not please himself but—Paul sets the thought in the idiom of Psalm 69—suffered the reproaches of those who reproached YHWH. Jesus is cast as the king who is humiliated by his zeal for the house of God (cf. John 2:17), who is taunted and assaulted by his enemies, and who cries out to God for deliverance.[8] This is an example of servanthood under opposition—it is advocated not as a matter of normal Christian behavior but as a way for the community to overcome the hostility of those who "reproach" the God of Israel. So as Paul says, the written text has direct relevance for a community that must learn to endure suffering, holding on to the hope of eventual vindication.

Troublemakers Who Do Not Serve Our Lord Christ: 16:17–20

In the closing paragraphs of the letter Paul appends to his numerous personal greetings a rather sharp and unexpected warning to the "brothers" to watch out for people who "cause divisions and create obstacles (*skandala*) contrary to the doctrine that you have been taught" (16:17). Their concern is not to serve Christ but to satisfy their "appetites" (*koiliai*); by "smooth talk and flattery they deceive the hearts of the naive," and Paul fears that they will subvert the obedience of the community. The eschatological dimension to this warning is clearly signaled in verse 20: "The God of peace will soon crush Satan under your feet. The grace of our Lord Jesus Christ be with you." The path of obedience that they have begun to walk will eventually culminate in the emphatic defeat of the power that now seeks to seduce them from their calling. But for now the grace of Jesus, who himself was bedeviled by the temptation—he also calls it a *skandalon* (Matt 16:23)—to avoid the way of suffering, will be with them. This is quite specifically the grace to resist the persuasive arguments of those who, in the corresponding language of Philippians 3:18–19, "walk as enemies of the cross of Christ," whose "god is their belly (*koilia*)," whose minds are "set on earthly things." Paul's concern is not for the general doctrinal integrity of the community: it is that the saints in Rome should

---

8. Ps 68:22 LXX ("for my thirst they gave me vinegar to drink") is alluded to in the crucifixion narratives (Matt 27:48; Luke 23:36; John 19:29); Ps 68:23 LXX is quoted by Paul at Rom 11:9–10.

be conformed to the image of the Son who suffered and was vindicated, which corresponds precisely with his appeal to the Philippians to imitate him in his determination to share in Christ's sufferings and become like him in his death, with the hope of attaining the resurrection from the dead (Phil 3:10, 17). The nature of the "teaching" (*didachēn*)—not mere "doctrine"—in which they have been instructed and which is contradicted by the troublemakers is suggested by the outcome that Paul highlighted in the introduction to the Letter, the "obedience of faithfulness," which, as 1 Thessalonians 1:6–10 shows, is always potentially a faithfulness in the face of suffering.

13

Reading Romans After Christendom

Paul sets out in Romans the argument that he has pursued with Jews and to a lesser extent Greeks across the eastern empire, from Jerusalem to Illyricum. It is an argument, ultimately, about the fate of the *oikoumenē*, the civilization of the ancient Mediterranean world, insofar as it was subject to the capricious, amoral, decadent, and ruthless gods and man-gods of Greco-Roman paganism. He believes that the resurrection of Jesus from the dead signaled the impending end of this world: God has fixed a day, a decisive moment in history, when he will judge the *oikoumenē* in righteousness—just as in the past he judged the Egyptians or the Assyrians or the Chaldeans—by a man whom he has appointed, when he will give to his Son the nations as an inheritance.

That prospect, however, has serious implications for a people that claims to have been uniquely chosen and gifted by this God to serve him. If God is to establish his righteousness—if he is to vindicate himself—with respect to the nations, he must first do something about the *unrighteousness* of Israel. He cannot judge the nations without first judging the people which, by virtue of its calling and its possession of the Law, should have been a kingdom of priests among all peoples, a light to the nations—a benchmark of righteousness. So wrath against the Greek world will be preceded by *wrath against Israel*, which in view of Paul's reliance on Old Testament narratives of judgment, in view of the teaching of Jesus about an impending catastrophe, and in the glaring light of hindsight, must be understood as a prophetic reference to the disastrous Judean revolt against Roman rule, the devastation of Jerusalem and the temple, and any repercussions that this was to have for Jews of the diaspora. Paul is convinced that God's patience with sinful Israel has run out and that the nation, as a consequence, faces destruction. But this creates another problem with respect to the righteousness—or rightness or integrity or credibility—of God: what has happened to his much vaunted loyalty to his chosen people? And in particular, what has happened to the seminal promise made to Abraham that his descendants would inherit the world?

The answer is that the resurrection of Jesus, the reality of which was dramatically impressed upon Paul on the road to Damascus, has highlighted an alternative way for the people of God to exist under the present difficult circumstances: the way of the Christ who embraces in himself the suffering of the people whom Paul was actively persecuting. The Law cannot guarantee the future of the people of God: indeed, it has come to the point where the Law pronounces an inescapable judgment on an incorrigible nation. But the story of Jesus's death and vindication had opened up a narrow and difficult path that would lead to life—a life anticipated in the liberating and transforming experience of the eschatological Spirit, the life of the age to come, the life of the future of the people of God beyond the protracted historical crisis of the wrath of God. Communities of Jews and Gentiles across the *oikoumenē* have been called by God *to stand for the fact that sooner or later he will show himself to be sovereign over the nations.* But if they are genuinely and consistently to stand as a sign of the righteousness of God, they will have to exercise a concrete and difficult trust in the groundbreaking event of Jesus's death and resurrection. They will have to emulate the faithfulness that confronted the most extreme and savage hostility, believing that Jesus's death has been accepted as an act of atonement for the sins of Israel and that the God who raised Jesus from the dead will likewise safeguard the future of the renewed, multiracial microcosm of the family of Abraham. This is the defining story that Habakkuk tells: when God acts to vindicate himself with respect first to Israel and then to the pagan empire by punishing unrighteousness, those who are righteous will live by their faithfulness.

That is the narrative by which the saints in Rome have to make sense of their existence and, in the coming years, interpret the tumultuous events that will come like a flood and a storm against the house of Israel, that will threaten the survival of these vulnerable fellowships at the heart of the darkness of pagan imperialism, and that will eventually sweep away the gods of the *oikoumenē*. If they are to play their part in this world-changing process as an acceptable "offering of the nations" to the God of Israel, they will need to develop new attitudes, new practices, a new self-understanding. If they are selfish, if they squabble, if they are torn apart by dissension and factionalism, if they become conceited about their new spiritual status, if they are careless about immorality in their midst, if their worship is compromised by idolatrous practices, if they despise the poor and the weak in faith, if they do not have a love that "bears all things, believes all things, hopes all things, endures all things" (1 Cor 13:7), if they harbor hatred towards their enemies, if they pick fights with the authorities, if they fail to grasp the utter seriousness of the eschatological moment that they face, if they fail to clothe themselves with the Lord Jesus Christ who was faithful to the point of death, then they will not survive the conflagration. They will be reduced to blackened ruins—like the temples of Luna, Hercules, and Jupiter on Nero's Day of Fire. So Paul writes to them somewhat boldly, in advance of his planned visit, to ensure that they understand who they are, why they have been called, and what it will take from them to fulfill the eschatological purpose that is signified by the phrase "offering of the nations."

Coming to Terms with Christendom

Reading Romans in this way leaves it as a stone firmly embedded in the cobbled road of a particular historical narrative. In itself it is as contingent—and therefore as circumscribed—as the letter which Jeremiah sent to the exiles in Babylon by the hand of Elasah the son of Shaphan and Gemariah the son of Hilkiah, explaining why they were there, how they were to live with the situation, and what they could expect to happen in a foreseeable and realistic future (Jer 29:1–23). The future that Paul has in mind in Romans is more complex and less sharply defined than the return from exile after seventy years that Jeremiah predicted, but it is no less foreseeable and realistic, and it is no less pertinent to the recipients of the letter.

We have now seen that future, and we have seen that it does not work—at least, not nearly as well as might have been hoped. The sovereignty of the risen Christ over the gods of the nations came to be concretely represented in the church's alliance with massive political, legal, cultural, and intellectual power. With hindsight we may have come to think of that relationship as regrettable, but it needs to be acknowledged as an integral part of the story of the people of God. The legitimization of Christianity by Constantine and its appropriation for imperial service cannot simply be dismissed as an aberration or irrelevancy—and in certain important respects must be seen as the proper fulfillment of eschatological expectations articulated in the New Testament, not least in Paul's Letter to the Romans. Just as the Jewish monarchy became a localized symbol for the kingship and kingdom of God, so in its imperial dimensions Christendom became a symbol for the global sovereignty of the one Creator God. Just as the land of Israel, in which the family of Abraham would be blessed, made fruitful, and would multiply, represented God's new creation in microcosm, so Christendom imagined that it might embody, on an imperial and potentially global scale, the eschatological reality of a new humanity in Christ, transcending the ingrained distinctions of the *oikoumenē* between Jew and Greek, Scythian and barbarian, slave and free, male and female. The narratives of Scripture were quickly translated into the potent idioms of Greek rationalism. A prophetic yearning for justice and peace was institutionalized in the political and legal structures of the empire. Most importantly, the gods of the ancient world were ousted, the rulers and authorities in the heavens were disarmed, and—in the non-idealized sense that must, in the first place, be given to biblical prophecy—every knee came to bow and every tongue confessed that Jesus, the faithful one, the anti-Caesar, was Lord, to the glory of God the Father.

Re-storying the Church

That has all now changed—not the lordship of Christ but the historical form through which it has been expressed for the last 1700 years. The alliance has collapsed, the paradigm has disintegrated: the *oikoumenē* no longer embodies in its political and social structures, its worship, its ways of thinking, or its worldview the sovereignty of the God of Israel invested in Jesus Christ. To the extent that the church has begun to reflect self-consciously on this massive realignment, the challenge it faces is one of re-establishing a plausible identity and purpose at the cultural margins. This is bound to be a multifaceted theological task, both conservative and inventive, both retrospective and progressive, both critical and reimaginative; but if we wish, in the first place, to remain in an exegetically defensible continuity with the biblical text, I think that we will have to learn to read the New Testament narratively and historically, as a text that interprets events and outcomes within the necessarily restricted outlook of short-sighted communities, immersed in a world and in a story very different to our own. In this way we will find in Scripture the theological and prophetic resources to understand and respond to the contingencies of the "eschatological" crisis that the post-Christendom church faces.

We only make things difficult for ourselves if we insist on framing the present task according to anachronistic narratives. We are not now living the story of the early church, whose "eschatology" was constructed (for the most part) in order to make sense of the two foreseeable horizons of wrath against the Jews and wrath against the Greco-Roman world, and to give vivid expression to the improbable hope that these small communities of refugee Jews and renegade Gentiles would one day inherit the world. Similarly, if we read Romans looking for material to support the conflicting theologies, the consolidated dogmatic positions, the prejudices and pronouncements, the creeds and anathemas of a paradigm that is passing away, we will not only continue to miss the situated argumentative dynamic of the letter; we may fail to grasp the fundamental seriousness of our own situation—that the integrity and rightness and credibility of the God and Father of our Lord Jesus Christ have been powerfully repudiated, impugned, by our culture, and that it is not at all clear that the story we tell will continue to make sense or that the people of God has a viable future. A narrative-historical, non-idealized reading of Romans teaches us that the question of the righteousness of God is a contingent one and may be revisited under very different circumstances.

The story of the people of God oscillates between formation and deformation, between crisis and consolidation, between destruction and renewal, between judgment and blessing. Israel came to exist in the Land as a new creation in microcosm, in fulfillment of the promise made to Abraham, only by way of a long journey that led from captivity to an unsympathetic foreign power, through a traumatic escape and painful wandering through the wilderness. The churches became an ecumenical people of God, an empire-wide expression of the sovereignty of the God of Israel, only by way of a long journey from captivity to Rome, through a traumatic redemption and a painful conflict with the obdurate gods of the *oikoumenē*. Similarly, refugees from the fallen city of Christendom are on a long journey from their captivity to oppressive, corrupting, demoralizing, destructive social and intellectual forces, through a traumatic self-examination, through disintegration and despair, through countless experiments in renewal and emergence, towards—one hopes—a new self-understanding, a new paradigm, a new mode of being, a new construction of what it means to be a credible new creation in the midst of the peoples and cultures of the earth. It is too early to guess what that new paradigm might look like, but we are certainly beginning, consciously and unconsciously, to re-imagine the place of the church in the world in keeping with the promise to Abraham, in the light of the hope that all things will be made new.

To my mind the template for this reoriented eschatology is the argument that underpins the entire biblical narrative—that the Creator steadfastly opposes the corruption of his creation by establishing the prospect of *new creation*.[1] The argument is both actually and prophetically, both concretely and symbolically, embodied in the long and continuing history of the family of Abraham, who was called from the start, not to "rescue the world from its plight"[2] or somehow put it to rights, but to be a distinct or holy microcosm, a small world in the midst of the nations, subject to the discipline and grace of the Creator. The motif shapes the hope of Israel's restoration (cf. Isa 51:1–3); it acquires novel ontological potential in the resurrection of Jesus; it has determined—for better or for worse—the dimensions and aspirations of the Christendom church; and it still defines for us the surprising hope of a final justice, a final victory over the destructive forces of sin and death, and a final making new of all things by which the Creator is restored to the heart of his creation.

When the existence and integrity of the people that is called to witness to this hope is threatened or put at risk, the story necessarily modulates—it becomes a story of faithfulness and suffering, martyrdom and glorification; and the people of God will no doubt, from time to time and from place to place, encounter levels of hostility that will give that motif a renewed potency. But for the Western church, and by and large for the exported global church, that is not the story in which we find ourselves and by which we must define our vocation. The threat to Western

1. This is the thesis of Perriman, *Re: Mission*.
2. Wright, *Justification*, 73, italics removed.

Christianity comes not from a repressive pagan imperialism that will herd defiant believers into the arenas to be slaughtered, but from a culture that has supreme confidence in its right—if not always its capacity—to define personal and social good, safeguard the health and prosperity of humanity, manage the world's material resources, process information and knowledge, determine the conditions and boundaries for truth, and regurgitate an endless stream of entertainments and distractions.

If we now proclaim to the world that God has raised Jesus from the dead, it is not because we are faced with the prospect of vicious political-religious suppression; it is because the challenge to the gods and rulers of the *oikoumenē* was always in principle also *a response to the corruptibility of the whole created order*; it was the beginning of a new creation. This is the narrative and biblical framework within which I think the various attempts to develop (and account for theologically) a practical ethical and social dimension to the church's purpose, which are so characteristic of evangelical and post-evangelical missional thinking today, need to be situated. The vocation of the people of God is to stand for the goodness and integrity of God's new creation—all that it means to be created, all that it means to be in relationship with the Creator, sustained by grace—in the midst of the nations and for the sake of the nations. Whenever that project is fundamentally threatened, by external or internal forces, as perhaps it is now, there is a need for judgment and salvation—and for the benchmark of righteousness to be recalibrated.

The Demonstration of the Righteousness of God

Our eschatology will have to address the question of whether God's patience is now running out with a global culture that has defied the Creator and been given over to unrestrained consumption, gross disparities of wealth and security, massive social and political violence, ideological manipulation on a monstrous scale, moral disorientation, and so on . . . How credibly we articulate this now conventional critique is another matter—even Paul's catalogue of the wrongs of paganism was derivative and populist; but we cannot read Romans without acknowledging the fact that his gospel and his call for the obedience of the nations provoked a confrontation that convulsed the world of classical paganism.

Our eschatology will also have to narrate the complicity of the church in the fundamental unrighteousness or unrightness of Western culture. The church must consider whether it can honestly claim to provide the benchmark of "righteousness," of creational integrity, as God's microcosm within the macrocosm of human society. We are bound to catch a disturbing glimpse of our own image in the mirror that we hold up to the world. So the question is whether it is still possible to posit in concrete terms an alternative good. Is the church genuinely capable of imagining and embodying a distinctive and holy way of being as a fully creational community, whose existence is determined by the Christ who was not only the firstborn martyr from the dead for the sake of Israel but the firstborn from all creation for the sake of the cosmos? Whether or not one agrees with Hart's depressing view of "the frozen mires and fetid marshes of modern Europe," where the loss of faith has produced a vast "metaphysical boredom" that has quite literally sapped the will to live, rendering "the imagination inert and desire torpid,"[3] we must surely conceive the task in much broader terms than re-evangelization or the revival of church-going. Whether or not we suppose that Christian America is on the same or some other path as post-Christian Europe, we must surely find ways to transcend the abysmal theological and ecclesial divisions left by the schisms of Christendom, we must surely break out from the mold of a narrow, complacent religiosity, and begin to narrate for ourselves a new future, to shape a new paradigm for the existence of the family of Abraham in the midst of the nations.

Romans teaches us, finally, that we must face the future on the basis of faith(fulness). In the first place, this is a *faith* like Abraham's, which *believes* the promise that God both secures and gives meaning to the future of his people. It may feel as though it is only a matter of time before the story of a Creator who has defined himself, justified himself, by raising his Son Jesus from the dead, gets completely over-written by the compelling, unanswerable narratives of modern life—narratives of scientific and technological achievement, narratives of psychic and genetic transformation, narratives of religious realignment, narratives of terror and insecurity, narratives of insidious and unaccountable corporate power, narratives of environmental destruction and catastrophic change. However sure we may be personally of the grounds of our faith, the historical perspective

3. Hart, *Atheist Delusions*, 16.

strongly suggests that Christianity as we have known it is on the wane—
and Scripture, as we have seen, trades in historical perspectives. Can we
do what Paul did and reformulate a trust in the God who called Abraham
that will give us hope for *our future*? But it is also a *faithfulness* such as
Habakkuk imagined would enable the righteous to survive the disorder
and distress, the clashing of nations, through which God would judge and
be justified. The early church looked to Jesus as the author and perfecter
of this faithfulness and struggled to emulate him for the sake of the future of the people of God. History has carried us beyond the orbit of this
critical story, but it remains the bright center of our solar system. What
endurance, what conviction, what determination, what *faithfulness* will it
now take in order for us to stay within its gravitational pull, as a people for
God's own possession? The night is far gone, the day is at hand . . . Not all
of Romans can be reduced to sane theologizing—something in it warns
us not to underestimate the challenges that lie ahead and the demands
that will be imposed on the churches if the righteousness of the Creator
God is to be demonstrated through the concrete life of faithful communities in our own foreseeable future.

Bibliography

Adams, Edward. *Constructing the World: A Study in Paul's Cosmological Language.* Studies of the New Testament and Its World. Edinburgh: T. & T. Clark, 2000.

Barrett, C. K. *The Epistle to the Romans.* Black's New Testament Commentaries. London: A. & C. Black, 1957.

Beasley-Murray, George R. *John.* Word Biblical Commentary 36. Dallas: Word, 1987.

Brown, Peter. *The Rise of Western Christendom: Triumph and Diversity, 200–1000 AD.* 2nd ed. Oxford: Blackwell, 1996.

Campbell, Douglas A. *The Deliverance of God: An Apocalyptic Rereading of Justification in Paul.* Grand Rapids: Eerdmans, 2009.

Charlesworth, James H. *The Old Testament Pseudepigrapha.* 2 vols. Garden City, NY: Doubleday, 1983–85.

Dunn, James D. G. *Romans 1–8.* Word Biblical Commentary 38A. Dallas: Word, 1998.

———. *Romans 9–16.* Word Biblical Commentary 38b. Dallas: Word, 1998.

Elliott, Neil. "The Apostle Paul and Empire." In *In the Shadow of Empire: Reclaiming the Bible as a History of Faithful Resistance,* edited by Richard A. Horsley, 97–116. Louisville: Westminster John Knox, 2008.

———. *The Arrogance of Nations: Reading Romans in the Shadow of Empire.* Paul in Critical Contexts. Minneapolis: Fortress, 2008.

Esler, Philip F. *Conflict and Identity in Romans: The Social Setting of Paul's Letter.* Minneapolis: Fortress, 2003.

Eusebius: The Church History. Translation and commentary by Paul L. Maier. Grand Rapids: Kregel, 1999, 2007.

Evans, Craig A. "Mark's Incipit and the Priene Calendar Inscription: From Jewish Gospel to Greco-Roman Gospel." *Journal of Greco-Roman Christianity and Judaism* 1 (2000) 67–81.

Fitzmyer, Joseph A. *Romans: A New Translation with Introduction and Commentary.* Anchor Bible 33. New York: Doubleday, 1993.

Gathercole, Simon J. *Where Is Boasting? Early Jewish Soteriology and Paul's Response in Romans 1–5.* Grand Rapids: Eerdmans, 2002.

Hart, David Bentley. *Atheist Delusions: The Christian Revolution and Its Fashionable Enemies.* New Haven, CT: Yale University Press, 2009.

Hays, Richard B. *Echoes of Scripture in the Letters of Paul.* New Haven: Yale University Press, 1989.

Käsemann, Ernst. *Commentary on Romans.* Translated and edited by Geoffrey W. Bromiley. Grand Rapids: Eerdmans, 1980.

Bibliography

Kirk, J. R. Daniel. *Unlocking Romans: Resurrection and the Justification of God.* Grand Rapids: Eerdmans, 2008.

Lincoln, Andrew T. *Ephesians.* Word Biblical Commentary 42. Dallas: Word, 1990.

Lopez, Davina C. *Apostle to the Conquered: Reimagining Paul's Mission.* Paul in Critical Contexts. Minneapolis: Fortress, 2008.

Moo, Douglas J. *The Epistle to the Romans.* New International Commentary on the New Testament. Grand Rapids: Eerdmans, 1996.

Perriman, Andrew C. *The Coming of the Son of Man: New Testament Eschatology for an Emerging Church.* Milton Keynes, UK: Paternoster, 2005.

————. *Re: Mission: Biblical Mission for a Post-Biblical Church.* Faith in an Emerging Culture. Milton Keynes, UK: Paternoster, 2007.

Piper, John. *The Future of Justification: A Response to N.T. Wright.* Wheaton, IL: Crossway, 2007.

Stowers, Stanley K. *The Diatribe and Paul's Letter to the Romans.* SBL Dissertation Series 57. Chico: Scholars Press, 1981.

Watson, Francis. *Paul, Judaism and the Gentiles: Beyond the New Perspective.* Rev. ed. Grand Rapids: Eerdmans, 2007.

Watts, John D. W. *Isaiah 1–33.* Word Biblical Commentary 24. Waco: Word, 1985.

Witherington, Ben III, and Darlene Hyatt. *Paul's Letter to the Romans: A Socio-Rhetorical Commentary.* Grand Rapids: Eerdmans, 2004.

Wright, N. T. "The Letter to the Romans." In *The New Interpreter's Bible,* edited by Leander E. Keck, 10:395–770. Nashville: Abingdon, 2002.

————. *Justification: God's Plan and Paul's Vision.* London: SPCK, 2009.

Index of Names

Abraham, 7, 9, 14, 19, 23, 26–27, 50, 60, 73, 75–76, 84, 87–88, 89n5, 90, 91n6, 92–95, 93n8, 101, 105n11, 116, 123, 127, 129, 132, 135–38, 136n7, 144, 152, 154–56, 158, 159
Adam, 100–106, 110, 114, 138
Adams, E., 91n7
Agrippa I, 54
Agrippa II, 25, 66
Antiochus Epiphanes, 40, 53, 58, 81, 86–87, 99, 101, 119
Augustus, 20, 55, 113
Barrett, C. K., 16n5
Beasley-Murray, G. R., 50n13
Brown, P., 11, 11n5, 121, 121n10
Caiaphas, 50
Campbell, D. A., 15, 15nn3–4, 19n6, 76n6, 77n7, 77n9, 108, 108n13
Claudius, 18, 23–24, 51, 55, 148
Constantine, 4, 6, 21, 56, 121, 154
Crossan, J. D., 22
David, 13, 17, 20, 49, 57, 68, 70, 87–89, 94, 110, 114, 133
Diocletian, 6
Dunn, J. D. G., 14n2, 20n9, 30n2, 32n5, 33n6, 42n3, 43n5, 44n6, 78n10, 91n6, 102n4, 103nn5–6, 116n2, 135n5, 136n7, 143n2, 147n6
Eleazar, 81
Elliott, N., 20–22, 20n7, 20nn10–11, 21n13, 30n2, 32n5, 35–36, 36n7, 42n1, 135, 135n6, 146, 147nn4–5
Esler, P. F., 75n5, 77n8
Eusebius, 6, 21–22, 120, 148
Evans, C. A., 20n7, 113n1

Fitzmyer, F. A., 31n4, 42n1, 43n5, 59n4
Gathercole, S. J., 94, 94n10
Georgi, D., 20
Hart, D. B., 1n1, 110, 110n17, 158, 158n3
Hays, R. B., 5n2, 88n3
Horsley, R. A., 22
Hyatt, D., 16n5, 20n7, 20n9, 29n1, 32n5, 75n2, 78, 78n12, 89n5, 93n8, 97n1, 98, 98n3, 118–19, 118n5, 144n3
Ignatius of Antioch, 120
Isidore of Pelusium, 11
Jeremias, J., 16
Jesus, 3, 7–10, 14, 16–17, 19, 21–22, 27, 29–32, 37, 39–40, 48–52, 54–56, 59–60, 62–64, 67, 69, 72–79, 81–84, 89, 93, 95–98, 100–102, 104–8, 110, 112–26, 129–30, 132, 135, 137–46, 148–49, 151–59
Josephus, 3, 25, 51, 54, 65–66, 133, 147
Judas Maccabeus, 80, 101
Käsemann, E., 16n5, 32n5
Kirk, J. R. D., 10n4, 21n12, 87nn1–2, 88n3, 91, 91n7, 93n8, 103, 103n7, 106, 106n12, 109, 109n16
Licinius, 6, 7, 21
Lincoln, A. T., 79n13
Lopez, D. C., 22n16, 22–28, 23nn17–19, 24nn20–22, 25nn23–26, 26nn27–28, 108, 108n15
Mattathias, 86–88, 93, 147
Moo, D. J., 44n6, 84n17, 119n7, 124, 124n12, 143n2
Moses, 17, 68, 90, 103, 127, 131, 146
Nebuchadnezzar, 37, 55

163

Index of Names

Index of Scripture References

Old Testament

Index of Scripture References

Ephesians

Philippians

Colossians

1 Thessalonians

2 Thessalonians

1 Timothy

2 Timothy

1 Peter

Hebrews

1 John

Revelation

Index of Ancient Sources